*Practical Handbook
of Canadian French*

✗ 3

Practical Handbook of Canadian French

SINCLAIR ROBINSON
DONALD SMITH

Manuel Pratique du Français Canadien

MACMILLAN OF CANADA
Toronto

Library of Congress Catalogue Card No. 73-8588

ISBN 0-7705-1027-2 Cloth
     0-7705-1028-0 Paper

Reprinted 1975, 1976

Printed and bound in Canada for the
Macmillan Company of Canada
70 Bond Street, Toronto

Table des Matières (Table of Contents)

Introduction

The study of French in English Canada has long been the subject of much discussion. Year after year, new courses, methods and theories are developed by teaching specialists. Yet, all too often, there is little resulting communication with the French-speaking community which is nearest to us: the French Canadians. Part of the problem has always been linguistic: courses developed in Canada have consistently ignored Canadian French. The persistent myths of pure "Parisian French" or "International French," and of the "French-Canadian patois," have destroyed students' motivation and discouraged teachers. It is our hope that the use of this handbook, by removing some of the mystery surrounding Canadian French, will help improve communication on the personal, individual level, between English and French Canadians.

Canadian French, like Canadian English, differs from the language of the mother country. We should no more expect French Canadians to speak "Parisian French" than ourselves to speak "Oxford English." A language exists not only in the tomes of the academics and grammarians, but also in the mouths of the people, where it lives and grows, and adapts itself to the ever-changing world around it. Through it the speakers of a linguistic community express their thoughts and emotions, and communicate with one another. A language is the result of history, of the movements and mingling of people, of geography and climate. More important, a language is the product of a culture, of a way of life, and at the same time its expression. It is the medium through which the heritage of a people is passed on from generation to generation. It is not surprising, then, that French in Canada should be different from the French of France, as different as are French Canadians themselves from their distant European cousins.

Canadian French is lively, colourful and imaginative; it has the same capacity for expressing the whole range of human concerns as any other tongue. After suffering for many years the attacks of language purists who wish to change the speech of a community of six million people to bring it more in line with that of another country, France, Canadian French has recently come into its own—in the theatre, on radio and television, in novels and poetry. The inherent qualities of the language are being discovered and exploited, to create expressive, beautiful works of art. What was merely "incorrect" has become relevant, alive and meaningful. Two important pioneer works demonstrate the richness of the French Canadian's language: the *Glossaire du parler français au Canada* of 1930, and Louis-A. Bélisle's *Dictionnaire général de la langue française au Canada*, published in 1957. There has awakened a new appreciation, a new awareness of the worth of Canadian French.[1] Soon, perhaps, French Canadians will follow English-speaking North Americans in recognizing their language as a distinctive variety of the European mother tongue.

Whatever may be the outcome of the present linguistic debates in Quebec, a knowledge of Canadian French remains, in our opinion, absolutely essential for all English Canadians wishing to communicate with their French-speaking neighbours. This handbook has been conceived as a practical aid to this communication, and as a supplement to existing French texts and courses. As such, it lists, along with their equivalents in "Standard French" and in English, those common words and expressions used in Quebec but whose form or meaning is rare or unknown in France, and hence not normally included in French courses in Canada.

The words are listed under various headings (sports, clothing, government, and so on) to facilitate consultation both for *active* use, where the reader wants to build up his vocabulary in a certain area, and for *passive* use, where the reader wants to know the meaning of a word encountered in a certain context. A compilation of general vocabulary and expressions follows these lists.

Often the reader will find several French-Canadian words with the same meaning. In these cases, usage may vary according to region, or according to the social background of the speaker. An indication of these differences was, of course, beyond the scope of this study, as a vast linguistic survey would be required. We have merely listed the

[1]See Henri Bélanger, *Place à l'homme: éloge du français québécois*, 1972.

variants in alphabetical order; all can be heard in Quebec, and all would most probably be understood.

Frequently, the French word is also used by French Canadians. Here again, the factors of education and background, of region and occupation, come into play. In certain instances, no exact equivalents exist for the Canadian French. The word is then explained or defined. In some cases, where the word refers to an object or concept foreign to France, the French column contains no equivalent.

We hope that the consultation and frequent use of this manual will open up to English-speaking Canadians, through the means of language, a world which is on their doorstep, but which has remained closed to them for too long.

The following people have read the manuscript and we would like to thank them for their invaluable help and advice: Huguette Béland-Ouellet, Henri Bélanger, Jacques Lajoie, Dominique Rosse and Jean-Jacques van Vlasselaer. Any errors or omissions are the sole responsibility of the authors.

Sinclair Robinson
Donald Smith
CARLETON UNIVERSITY

*Practical Handbook
of Canadian French*

A Note to the Reader

This handbook does not purport to be complete. The authors have attempted to give the most useful words and expressions in Canadian French which differ from the French normally taught in Canada. The reader is invited to add to the manual from his own experience.

French-Canadian words and expressions listed in this handbook are either unknown or have a limited usage in France. When used in France, they are often considered either very colloquial or archaic. In many cases, the French words or expressions are also used in Quebec.

The authors have endeavoured, wherever possible, to give English equivalents which accurately reflect the very colloquial tone of certain French-Canadian words or expressions. The words given as equivalents in France may often be more literary or less colourful than the Quebec words, but these are nevertheless the usual words taught in French courses in English Canada.

Avis au lecteur

Ce manuel n'est pas exhaustif. Les auteurs ont essayé d'y mettre les mots canadiens-français les plus courants et qui diffèrent du français de France. Les auteurs suggèrent au lecteur de prendre note lui-même d'autres mots canadiens qui ne sont pas dans ce manuel.

Les mots et expressions canadiens qui figurent dans ce manuel sont soit inconnus soit peu répandus en France. Souvent, ces mots seraient ressentis comme étant populaires ou archaïques en France.

Dans plusieurs cas, les mots et expressions français se disent également au Canada.

Les auteurs ont essayé dans la mesure du possible de donner des équivalents anglais qui refléteraient le ton populaire de certains mots ou expressions canadiens-français.

Les mots donnés comme des équivalents français sont souvent moins familiers que les mots québécois, mais il reste que ce sont eux qu'on enseigne habituellement au Canada anglais.

Abréviations (Abbreviations)

adj.: adjectif
esp.: especially
(f): féminin
(m): masculin
(pl): pluriel
qch: quelque chose
qn: quelqu'un
(sing): singulier
s.o.: someone
sth.: something

Cuisine

Aliments et Repas (Food and Meals)

Canada	France	
arachide, pinotte (f)	*cacahouète*	peanut
beurre d'arachides, de pinottes (croquant)	*pâté de cacahouètes*	peanut butter (crunchy)
croquant aux arachides (m)		peanut brittle
assiette froide (f)	*assiette anglaise*	cold plate
atacas, atocas (m), canneberges (f)	*sorte d'airelle*	cranberries
baglosse, bagosse (f)	*boisson de fabrication clandestine*	moonshine
barbecue (poulet, etc.)	*à la broche*	barbecue (chicken)
soupe au barlerie, barley (f)	*soupe à l'orge*	barley soup
barre, palette de chocolat (f)	*tablette de chocolat*	chocolate bar
se batcher	*faire sa propre cuisine*	to do one's own cooking, to bach it
beigne (m, f)	*beignet*	doughnut
baloné (m)	*mortadelle, saucisson de Bologne*	bologna
beurrée (f)	*tartine; tartinage*	bread and butter, bread and jam; spread
beurrer	*étaler de la confiture, etc., sur une tartine*	to spread
bière d'épinette (f)	*sapinette*	spruce beer, root beer
binnes, fèves au lard (f)	*haricots au four*	pork 'n beans
biscuits mélangés, biscuits mêlés (m)	*biscuits assortis*	mixed biscuits

Canada	France	
biscuits soda	*craquelins, crackers*	soda biscuits
blé d'Inde (m)	*maïs*	corn
bleuet (m)	*myrtille*	blueberry
boisson (f)	*boisson alcoolique*	drink (alcoholic)
bonne, bonnse, bun (f)	*brioche*	bun
bonne, bonnse, bun, brioche (f)	*petit pain*	roll
boston steak (m)	*romsteck*	Boston Steak
brioche (f), muffin (m)	*gâteau*	muffin
broue (f)	*mousse*	foam, froth (on beer)
butterscotch (m)	*caramel au beurre*	butterscotch
cachou (m)	*noix d'acajou*	cashew
café, thé à la glace, café, thé froids (m)	*café glacé ...*	iced tea, coffee
cannages (m)	*conserves*	preserves
canner, encanner	*mettre en conserve*	to preserve, to can, put up
caribou (m)	*boisson canadienne (vin et whisky)*	French-Canadian drink (wine and whisky)
huile de castor (f)	*huile de ricin*	castor oil
casse-croûte (m)	*collation, snack*	snack
castonade (f), sucre brun (m)	*cassonade*	brown sugar
catchope, ketchoppe, ketchup (m)	*sauce aux tomates*	ketchup
céréale (f)	*porridge, corn flakes, etc.*	cereal (hot, cold), flakes
cerises de France (f)	*grosses cerises, bigarreaux*	large red cherries
cerises à grappes	*cerises de Virginie, petites cerises*	small red cherries, chokecherries
cheddar (m)	*fromage canadien*	cheddar
chiard (m)	*viande hachée*	ground meat

Canada	France	
chien-chaud (m)	*hot-dog*	hot dog
chips, croustilles (f)	*pommes de terre chips*	potato chips
chop (f)	*côtelette*	chop (pork, etc.)
cipaille, cipâte (m)	*pâté de viande canadien*	meat pie (meat and vegetables)
club steak (m)	*faux filet*	club steak
coke (m)	*coca*	coke
cole-slaw (m), salade de chou (f)	*salade de chou cru*	coleslaw
clamme (f)	*bricarde, coque*	clam
coconotte (m)	*noix de coco*	cocoanut
confiture aux fraises, aux bleuets (f)	*confiture de fraises . . .*	strawberry, blueberry jam
conistache, cornstache (m)	*amidon de maïs*	corn starch
cornet, cône (m) (de crème à glace)	*glace*	(ice cream) cone
cossetarde (f)	*flan*	custard
coton (m)	*fane; tige*	husk (of corn), sprout (of potatoes)
crémer	*glacer*	to ice
crémage (m)	*glace*	icing
crème de blé (f)	*semoule*	cream of wheat
crème à (la) glace, crème en glace, crème glacée (f)	*glaces*	ice cream
crème glacée molle	*glace plus molle que la glace ordinaire*	soft ice cream
cretons, gortons (m)	*rillettes*	potted minced of pork drippings
croquignole (f)	*beignet cuit dans de la graisse*	homemade French-Canadian doughnut cooked in shortening
curry (m)	*cari*	curry
cuisinette (f)	*petite cuisine*	kitchenette
débiter	*vider; dépecer*	to clean, to cut up a bird

3

Canada	France	
dégréyer, ôter (la table)	*débarrasser la table*	to clear the table
déjeuner (m)	*petit déjeuner*	breakfast
déjeuner	*prendre le petit déjeuner*	to have breakfast
démêler	*délayer*	to mix (flour with milk)
dills (m)	*cornichons au fenouil*	dill pickles
dîner (m)	*déjeuner*	lunch, dinner
dîner	*déjeuner*	to have lunch, to have dinner (noon hour)
dîner d'affaires	*déjeuner à un prix spêcial*	businessmen's luncheon
draffe (f)	*pression*	draft (beer)
une draffe	*un demi*	a draft
eau gazeuse, liqueur (douce) (f)	*boisson gazeuse (sans alcool)*	soft drink, pop
écaille (f)	*coquille (oeuf), écale (noix)*	shell (egg, nut)
écailler	*écaler*	to shell (nuts)
égousser	*écosser*	to shell (peas, beans)
enfirouâper qch.	*s'empiffrer de qch.*	to gobble sth. down, stuff oneself with sth.
épiceries (f)	*provisions*	groceries
éplucher, plumer	*peler*	to peel
éplure (f)	*pelure*	peeling
essence (f), goût (m)	*parfum, saveur*	flavour
évaporé (lait, etc.)	*concentré, condensé*	evaporated (milk, etc.)
faire l'ordinaire	*faire la cuisine*	to cook
fâr (m)	*farce*	stuffing, dressing
tarte à la farlouche, à la ferluche (f)	*tarte faite de mélasse, de farine, et de raisins secs*	French-Canadian pie made of sugar, flour and molasses
fesse de porc; fesse de veau (f)	*jambon; quartier de veau*	ham; haunch of veal

Canada	France	
fève (f)	*haricot*	bean
fèves jaunes, petites fèves	*haricots jaunes*	wax beans
fèves de Lima	*gros pois*	Lima beans
fèves rouges	*haricots rouges*	kidney beans
fèves soya	*pois chinois*	soybeans
fèves vertes	*haricots verts*	green beans
fleur (f)	*farine*	flour
forçure (f)	*fressure; foie*	pluck; liver
fromage cottage (m)	*fromage de caillé, de maison*	cottage cheese
fromage en grains	*fromage égoutté non pressé*	curd cheese, curds
fruitages (m)	*fruits (des champs)*	wild berries
fudge, fondant (m)	*fondant au chocolat*	fudge
fudgesicle (m)	*sucette au fondant congelé*	fudgesicle
gadelle (f)	*groseille*	gooseberry, red currant
gadelle noire	*cassis*	black currant
gâteau éponge (m)	*gâteau de Savoie, de mousseline*	sponge cake
gâteau des anges	*sorte de gâteau de Savoie*	angel cake
ginger-ale (f)	*boisson gazeuse au gingembre*	ginger ale
gomme balloune (f)	*gomme à bulles*	bubble gum
gomme à mâcher	*chewing-gum*	chewing-gum
gorlot (m), jarnotte (f)	*petite pomme de terre en forme de grelot*	small round potato
goûter quelque chose, goûter bon	*avoir le goût de quelque chose, avoir un bon goût*	to taste of something, to taste good
grévé (m)	*jus, sauce*	gravy
gros gin (m)	*sorte de genièvre*	Dutch gin
une grosse	*une grande bouteille de bière*	a large bottle of beer
gruau (m), soupane (f)	*porridge*	porridge, hot cereal
guernaille, tiraille, tirasse (f)	*tendon, tirant*	gristle

Canada	France	
haddeck (m)	*aiglefin*	haddock
hamburger (m)	*boeuf haché; sandwich au boeuf haché*	hamburger
instantané (café, etc.)	*soluble*	instant (coffee, etc.)
jello (m)	*gelée*	jello
jujube (m)	*pâté de fruits*	jujube, gumdrop
julienne (f)	*frite longue et mince*	shoestring potato
lait battu, brassé, fouetté (m)	*mélange de lait et de "crème glacée"*	milk shake
lait de beurre	*petit lait*	buttermilk
lait deux pour cent	*lait partiellement écrémé*	2% milk
lait écrémé		skim milk
lait homogénéisé		homogenized milk
moitié-moitié (m)		half-and-half
lard (m)	*saindoux*	lard
lard salé	*petit salé*	salt pork
lunch (m)	*déjeuner*	lunch
luncher	*déjeuner*	to have lunch
mâchemâlo (m)	*guimauve*	marshmallow
maïs soufflé, popcorn (m)	*maïs grillé, éclaté*	popcorn
gros mangeux (m)	*gros mangeur*	glutton
marmelade (f)	*confiture d'oranges*	marmalade
marinades (f)	*pickles*	pickles
médium	*à point*	medium
mélange à gâteau (m)	*gâteau préparé*	cake mix
mettre la table	*mettre le couvert*	to set the table
mordée (f)	*bouchée*	bite, mouthful
motton (m)	*grumeau, granule*	lump (in cereal, etc.)
nanane, nénane (m)	*bonbons*	candy, goodies
nectarine (f)	*brugnon*	nectarine
noix mélangées (f)	*mélange de cacahouètes, de pacanes, etc.*	mixed nuts

Canada	France	
(nourriture) chargeante	*indigeste*	hard to digest (food)
oeuf battu, egg-nog (m)	*lait de poule*	eggnog
oeuf frit	*oeuf sur le plat*	fried egg
un pain	*du pain de mie*	loaf of bread
pain blanc	*pain de mie*	white bread
pain de blé entier	*pain complet*	brown bread, whole wheat bread
pain brun	*pain bis*	dark bread, brown bread
pain doré	*pain perdu*	French toast
pain français	*baguette*	French bread stick
pain sandwich	*pain de mie pour faire des sandwichs*	sandwich bread
paparmane (f)	*pastille de menthe*	peppermint
patate (f)	*pomme de terre*	potato
patates bouillies	*pommes de terre à l'anglaise, à l'eau*	boiled potatoes
patates au four, en chemise	*pommes de terre au four*	baked potatoes
patates frites	*frites*	French fries
patates au gratin	*coquille de pommes de terre au gratin*	scalloped potatoes
patates pilées	*purée de pommes de terre*	mashed potatoes
patates rôties, patates fricassées	*pommes de terre frites dans la poêle*	fried potatoes
patates sucrées	*patates (douces)*	sweet potatoes
pâté (aux bleuets, etc.) (m)	*petite pâtisserie aux confitures recouverte d'une pâte*	tart
pâté chinois (m)	*hachis parmentier*	shepherd's pie
pâtisseries françaises (f)	*pâtisseries assorties*	French pastry
pécane (m, f)	*pacane*	pecan
pelure (f)	*peau (banane), écorce (orange)*	peel, peeling, skin (banana, orange)

Canada	France	
petit blanc (m)	*petit verre d'alcool*	shot (of alcohol)
une petite	*petite bouteille de bière*	pint (small bottle of beer)
piger à même le plat	*se servir à même un plat commun*	to take food from a common bowl, etc.
platée (de viande, etc.) (f)	*assiettée*	plate (of meat, etc.)
pois verts (m)	*petits pois*	green peas
ponce (f)	*boisson (chaude) faite avec du miel, citron, whisky ou gin, pour guérir un rhume*	toddy
popsakeule, popsicle (m)	*sucette aux boissons gazeuses*	popsicle
(sucre en) poudre (f)	*sucre à glacer*	icing sugar
poudre à pâte (f)	*baking-powder, levure (d'Alsace)*	baking powder
poutine (f)	*pouding*	pudding
poutine râpée (f)	*mélange de pommes de terre et de viande*	(Acadian) dish of meat and potatoes
prune séchée (f)	*pruneau*	prune
pruneau (m)	*grosse prune*	large plum
queue (d'oignon, d'échalote) (f)	*tige*	(onion, shallot) tail, top
ragôut de pattes (m)	*ragôut aux pattes de cochon*	French-Canadian pigs' feet stew
raisin (m)	*raisin sec*	raisin
raisins (m, pl)	*grappes de raisin, raisin (m, sing)*	grapes
ravel, réveul (m)	*esquimau*	ice cream bar
reliche, relish (m, f)	*sauce aux cornichons*	relish
repas complet (m)	*repas avec tous les services*	full-course meal
repas léger	*collation*	light meal, snack
restants (m)	*restes*	leftovers
rib-steak (m)	*côte de boeuf, entrecôte*	rib steak

Canada	France	
robine (f)	*alcool méthylique; tord-boyaux, mauvaise boisson*	rubbing alcohol; cheap liquor, rot-gut, hooch, rubby
ronde (f)	*gîte à la noix*	round (of beef)
rôti de boeuf (m)	*rosbif*	roast beef
rôtie, toast, tôsse (f)	*pain grillé, toast (m)*	piece of toast
rye (m)	*whisky canadien*	rye
salade (f)	*laitue*	lettuce
sandwich (f)	*sandwich (m)*	sandwich
de la saucisse	*des saucisses*	sausages
set de vaisselle (m)	*ensemble de vaisselle*	set of dishes
shortening (m)	*graisse alimentaire*	shortening
sirop d'érable (m)	*maple syrup*	maple syrup
smoked meat (m), viande fumée (f)	*boeuf fumé*	smoked meat
soda à pâte (m)	*bicarbonate de soude*	baking soda
sonnedé, sundae (m)	*glace aux fruits couverte d'une sauce sucrée, ice-cream*	sundae
soupe à la gourgane (f)	*soupe aux haricots*	bean soup (from the Saguenay area)
souper (m)	*dîner*	supper
souper	*dîner*	to have supper, to have dinner (evening)
du spaghetti	*des spaghettis*	spaghetti
spareribs (f)	*côtes découvertes*	spareribs
spencer steak (m)	*faux filet*	spencer steak
steak (m)	*bifteck*	steak
steak haché	*boeuf haché*	ground steak
suçon (m)	*sucette*	sucker, lollipop
sucrages (m, pl)	*sucreries*	goodies, candies
sucre blanc (m)	*sucre raffiné*	white sugar
surloin, surlonge (m)	*romsteck*	sirloin
surette (f)	*bonbon acidulé*	lemon drop, sour candy

Canada	France	
tangerine (f)	*mandarine, orange d'Algérie*	tangerine
tarte au sucre (f)	*tarte à la mélasse et au sucre*	French-Canadian sugar pie
t-bone (m)	*aloyau*	T-bone
tenderloin (m)	*filet*	tenderloin
tête en (de) fromage, tête fromagée (f)	*fromage de tête*	headcheese
tête de violon (f)	*légume de Nouvelle-Ecosse*	fiddlehead
tire (f)	*sirop de sucre*	pull-candy, taffy, molasses candy
tire-éponge	*bonbon au sirop de sucre*	sponge toffee
tire sur la neige	*"tire" faite sur la neige*	maple taffy (on the snow)
tourtière (f)	*pâté à la viande; tarte*	French-Canadian meat pie; pie
un 12 onces, un flasse, un (petit) mickey		a mickey, a 12-ouncer
un 26 onces		a 26-ouncer
un 40 onces		a 40-ouncer
vinaigrette au fromage bleu (f)	*vinaigrette au roquefort*	blue cheese salad dressing
vinaigrette française		French dressing

Dans la cuisine (In the kitchen)

bâleur (m)	*chaudron*	boiler
batteur (m)	*moussoir*	egg beater
blendeur (m)	*mélangeur, moulinette*	blender
boîte à lunch (f)	*gamelle*	lunch pail
bombe (f), canard (m)	*bouilloire*	kettle
bouteille (f)	*biberon*	feeding bottle, baby bottle

Canada	France	
cabaret (m)	*plateau*	tray
chassepanne, chassepinte (f)	*casserole*	saucepan
cocotier (m)	*coquetier*	egg cup
congélateur (m), glacière (f)	*freezer, frigorifique de ménage*	home-freezer, deep freeze
couloir (m), passe (f)	*tamis*	strainer
coutellerie (f)	*couteaux, fourchettes, cuillers*	cutlery, utensils
cuillère à thé (f)	*cuillère à café, petite cuillère*	teaspoon
cuillère à table	*cuillère à soupe*	tablespoon
élément, rond (m)	*foyer*	(stove) element
essuie-mains, linge (m)	*torchon*	dishtowel
fourneau (m)	*four*	oven
fridge, frigidaire (m)	*frigo*	fridge, refrigerator
plat de granit (m)	*casserole émaillée*	glazed pot
hache, tranche (f)	*couperet*	meat chopper
lavier, renvoi d'eau, signe (m)	*évier, lavabo*	sink
linge (m)	*lavette*	dishcloth
malaxeur (m), mixette (f)	*mixeur*	mixmaster
moulin à viande (m)	*hache-viande*	meat grinder
nettoyeur (m)	*nettoyant, détergent*	cleaner
panne (f)	*lèchefrite; poêle*	broiler; frying pan
panner	*faire frire dans une poêle*	to fry in a pan
pantrie (f), pènetré (m)	*dépense, garde-manger*	pantry
papier d'aluminium, papier de plomb (m)	*papier d'étain, d'argent*	(tin) foil
papier ciré	*papier paraffiné*	wax paper
pic (m), pique (f) à glace	*piolet*	ice pick

Canada	France	
pilon à patates (m)	*presse-purée*	potato masher
plat (m)	*casserole*	saucepan, pot
plat à vaisselle (m)	*bassine à vaisselle*	dishpan
poêle (m), tôle (f)	*cuisinière*	stove, range
poêlon (m)	*poêle*	frying pan
presto (m)	*autoclave, autocuiseur*	pressure cooker
renverser (l'eau renverse)	*se sauver*	to boil over
rôtisserie (f)	*barbecue*	barbecue
rouleau à pâte (m)	*rouleau à pâtisserie*	rolling pin
soucoupée (f)	*contenu d'une soucoupe*	saucerful
suce (f)	*sucette, tétine*	(baby) pacifier, nipple
toasteur (m)	*grille-pain*	toaster
torchon (m)	*linge à plancher*	rag (for the floor)
vaisseau (m)	*récipient, casserole*	container, pan

Au restaurant (In a restaurant)

breuvage (m)	*boisson non alcoolique servie avec les repas*	beverage
club sandwich (m)		club sandwich
facture (f), slip (m)	*addition*	bill, check
menu (m)	*carte*	menu
tarte à la mode (f)	*tarte avec une glace*	pie à la mode
order, ordonner	*commander*	to order
ordre (m)	*commande*	order
une patate	*une commande de frites*	an order of French fries

Canada	France	
pas payeux	*pas généreux*	tight (with money)
reliche-moutarde	*avec du condiment et de la moutarde*	with mustard and relish
salle à dîner	*salle à manger*	dining room
smokeméte (m)	*sandwich au boeuf fumé*	smoked meat (sandwich)
spécial du jour (m)	*plat du jour*	(the day's) special
(hot-dog) stimé	*(hot-dog) vapeur*	steamed (hot dog)
tip (m)	*pourboire*	tip
tipper	*laisser un pourboire*	to tip
tipper qn	*donner un pourboire à qn*	to tip s.o.
toaster	*griller*	to toast (sandwich, etc.)
payer la traite	*payer la tournée*	to pay the round
traiter qn	*offrir (un verre, etc.) à qn*	to treat s.o.

Boisson (Drinking)

avoir le bloc, le mal de bloc	*avoir la gueule de bois*	to have a hangover
être en boisson	*être ivre*	to be drunk
brosser	*boire à l'excès*	to hit the bottle
brosseur (m)	*ivrogne*	drunkard
prendre une brosse, partir sur une brosse, en revirer une ...	*s'enivrer, prendre une cuite*	to get drunk, go on a spree
chaud, e	*ivre*	drunk
chaudasse	*un peu ivre*	tipsy
correct, e	*dessoûlé*	sober, sobered up
se déranger	*s'enivrer*	to get drunk
être en fête	*être ivre*	to be loaded
gazé, e	*saoul*	drunk
se mouiller le gorgoton	*boire*	to drink, to wet one's whistle

13

Canada	France	
pacté, e	*ivre*	drunk, plastered
se pacter (le beigne, la fraise)	*s'enivrer*	to get drunk, plastered
parti pour la gloire	*saoul*	drunk
partir sur une balloune, prendre une balloune, virer une balloune	*se saouler*	to get loaded
partir sur une fripe	*se saouler*	to get drunk
prendre un coup	*prendre un verre; aimer boire*	to have a shot; to like drinking
se rincer le dalot	*se rincer la dalle*	to wet one's whistle
robiner	*boire à l'excès*	to be a drunk
robineux (m)	*ivrogne*	drunk; wino, rubby
soûlade (f)	*soûlerie*	binge, spree
soûlon (m)	*soûlard*	drunk, drunkard

Maison, Bâtiments (Home, Buildings)

Demeure (Residence)

Canada	France	
accommodation (f)	logement, capacité de logement	accommodation
accommoder	loger	to accommodate
allonge, shède (f)	annexe; remise, hangar	addition; shed
appartements (m, pl)	pièces	rooms
donner un avis	. . . préavis	to give notice
bacheleur, bachelor (m)	garçonnière	bachelor (apartment)
bas-côté (m)	appentis	porch or shelter attached to house
bâtisse (f)	édifice, building	building
bloc à appartements (m)	maison de rapport	apartment house, building
maison en bois rond	maison en rondins	log house
bungalow (m)	maison à un étage avec vérandas	bungalow
cabane (f), trou (m)	baraque, logement minable	hole, dump
cabane à chien (f)	niche à chien	doghouse
cabines pour touristes (f)	maisonnettes pour voyageurs	tourist cabins
camp, camp d'été (m)	maison de campagne, chalet	cottage, camp, summer cottage
carport (m)	garage sans murs	carport
chambrer	louer une chambre	to room
chambreur (m)	personne qui loge à un domicile sans y prendre ses repas	roomer
colonial, e	de style anglais	colonial (furniture)
conciergerie (f)	immeuble avec chambres à louer et un concierge	housekeeping apartments, apartment house

Canada	France	
condominium (m)	*série de maisons "attachées", copropriété*	condominium
développement (m)	*quartier résidentiel*	development
développer (des lots, etc.)	*exploiter . . .*	to develop (lots, etc.)
duplex (m)	*maison à 2 étages*	duplex
bas- (de) duplex	*partie inférieure de cette maison*	lower duplex
haut- (de) duplex	*partie supérieure de cette maison*	upper duplex
duplex double, quadruplex (m)	*maison à 2 étages et à 4 logis*	quadruplex
enclos public (m)	*fourrière*	dog pound
espace de bureau (m) (à louer)	*locaux de bureau*	office space (for rent)
flat (m)	*plain-pied, petit appartement*	flat
foyer pour personnes âgées (m), maison de vieillards (f)	*maison de retraite, hospice de vieillards*	home for the aged, senior citizens' home
location (f)	*emplacement*	location
logement à prix modique (m)	*habitation à loyer modique (H.L.M.)*	low-rental housing
logis (m)	*demeure*	home, house
loyer (m)	*appartement*	apartment
être à loyer	*être locataire*	to be a tenant
maison canadienne, québécoise (f)	*maison de style "canadien"*	old style French-Canadian house
maison de chambres	*hôtel garni*	rooming house
maison coloniale	*maison préfabriquée de style "colonial"*	colonial home
maison détachée (semi-détachée)	*maison (jumelle)*	detached home (semi-detached)
maison mi-étage	*maison d'un étage et demi*	one and a half storey house
maison mobile	*caravane luxueuse*	mobile home
maison modèle	*maison témoin*	model home
maison de pension, pension privée (f)	*pension*	boarding house

Canada	France	
maison privée	*maison particulière*	private home
maison de repos	*maison de retraite*	rest home
maison de ville	*hôtel*	town house
multifamilial, e	*pour plusieurs familles*	multi-family (dwelling)
pensionner	*louer une chambre avec pension*	to board
place (f)	*endroit*	place (apt., room)
privé, e (balcon, chambre, plage, stationnement, etc.)	*(balcon, chambre, parking) particulier, ère*	private (balcony, room, beach, parking, etc.)
propre	*en bon état*	clean (when selling an apartment, etc.)
propriété (f)	*terrain avec ou sans maison*	property
propriété commerciale, industrielle	*local commercial, industriel*	commercial, industrial property
résidence (f)	*domicile, maison, demeure*	residence
rester	*demeurer*	to live (in a place)
roulotte (f)	*caravane*	house trailer
tente-roulotte	*remorque de camping*	tent trailer, camping trailer
secteur domiciliaire (m)	*quartier résidentiel*	residential area
split-level (m)	*maison à paliers*	split level
subdivision (f)	*quartier en banlieue*	subdivision
suite (f)	*appartement, local, porte*	suite
triplex (m)	*maison à trois étages ou à trois logis*	triplex
un troisième (quatrième, etc.)	*"appartement" au troisième étage . . .*	third (fourth, etc.) storey apt.
unifamilial, e	*pour une famille*	single-family (dwelling)
unités (f,pl)	*chambres, pièces*	units (in an apartment building)

Dans la Maison (In the House)

Canada	France	
air conditionné	*climatisation, climatisé*	air conditioning, air-conditioned
avoir l'aqueduc	*avoir l'eau courante*	to have running water
arborite (m)	*lamelle décorative*	arborite
armoire (à butin) (f)	*placard*	closet
armoire en coin, coinçon (m)	*encoignure*	corner cupboard
arrimé, e	*en ordre, propre*	neat, tidy (house)
bain (m)	*baignoire*	bathtub
balai (m)	*vergette*	whisk
balayeuse (f)	*aspirateur*	vacuum cleaner
faire le barda	*faire le ménage*	to do the housework
barrer	*fermer à clef*	to lock
bas (m)	*rez-de-chaussée, étage inférieur*	first floor, lower floor
bassine (f)	*pot de chambre*	bedpan, pot
bassinette, bazinette (f)	*moïse*	bassinet
ber (m)	*berceau*	cradle, crib
blagne, bligne (m), toile (f)	*store*	blind
bois de boutte, bois de poêle (m)	*bois à brûler*	firewood
bois de corde	*bois de chauffage*	cordwood
bois de finition	*bois de première qualité*	finishing wood
bois franc	*bois dur*	hardwood
bois mou	*bois blanc*	softwood
boisé, e	*lambrissé*	panelled
boîte d'entrée, à fusibles (f)	*coupe-circuit*	circuit breaker, fuse box
bol (de toilette) (m)	*cuvette*	toilet bowl
bourrier (m)	*balayures*	sweepings
bras (m)	*garde-fou*	railing
broyeur (m)	*"broyeur" (dans l'évier) pour les ordures*	garbage disposal

Canada	France	
brûleur à l'huile (m)	*chaudière*	oil burner
bureau (de chambre) (m)	*commode*	chest of drawers, dresser
bureau simple, double . . .	*commode à une rangée . . .*	single, double chest of drawers
cabaneau, cabanon (m)	*placard, armoire*	cupboard, locker, cubbyhole
cabinet (à boisson, d'appareil) (m)	*bar; coffret, ébénisterie*	bar; cabinet, case
cadre (m)	*tableau*	hanging, painting, picture
calorifère (m)	*système de chauffage; radiateur*	heating system; radiator
catalogne (f)	*couverture, tapis rayés*	French-Canadian blanket or rug
cave (f), soubassement (m)	*sous-sol*	basement
cavreau (m)	*réduit sous l'escalier; petit entrepôt pour légumes, etc.*	storage room, cupboard under stairs, fruit cellar
centre de table (m)	*surtout*	centrepiece (for table)
(chaise) berçante (f)	*rocking-chair, fauteuil à bascule*	rocking chair
chaise haute	*chaise de bébé*	high chair
chambre (f)	*bureau, salle, pièce*	room, office
chambre double, simple; chambre de bain, de toilette	*chambre à deux lits, à un lit; salle de bain*	double, single room; bathroom
chambre de lavage, salle de lavage	*laverie*	laundry room
chambre des maîtres, grande chambre	*chambre principale*	master bedroom
champlure (f)	*robinet*	tap
chandelle (f)	*bougie*	candle
châssis (m)	*fenêtre*	window
châssis double	*contre-fenêtre*	storm window
chaufferette, truille (f)	*(petit) réchaud*	(portable, small) heater

Canada	France	
chesterfield (m)	*canapé (capitonné)*	chesterfield
clabord (m)	*bois ou aluminium à clin*	wood or aluminum siding
cloche (f)	*sonnette*	(door) bell
cocron, coqueron (m)	*petite pièce mal entretenue; placard dérobé*	small untidy room; concealed cupboard
cogner	*frapper*	to knock (on the door)
coiffeuse-vanité (f)	*coiffeuse*	vanity table
commode simple, double (f)	*commode à une rangée . . .*	single, double chest of drawers
confortable (m)	*édredon*	(eiderdown) comforter, quilt
connecter, ploguer	*brancher*	to plug in
déconnecter, déploguer, disconnecter	*débrancher*	to unplug
corniche (f)	*tablette de cheminée*	mantelpiece
courant direct (m)	*courant continu*	direct current
couverte (f)	*couverture*	blanket, cover
davenport (m)	*divan-lit*	davenport
débarrer	*ouvrir*	to unlock
deux-par-quatre (m)	*planche, deux pouces sur quatre pouces*	two-by-four
dînette (f)	*petite salle à manger, ses meubles*	dinette, dinette furniture
draperies, tentures (f)	*rideaux*	curtains, drapes
époussette (f), pleumas (m)	*plumeau*	(feather) duster, whisk
(tout) équipé, fourni	*avec réfrigérateur, cuisinière, etc.*	(all) equipped
premier étage (m)	*rez-de-chaussée*	ground floor, first floor
deuxième étage	*premier étage*	second floor
étude (f)	*bureau*	study
fausse-porte (f)	*contre-porte*	storm door, screen door

Canada	France	
filage (m)	*câblage*	wiring (appliance)
filerie (f)	*canalisations*	wiring (house)
fini, e (cave finie, etc.)	*meublé et décoré*	finished (basement etc.)
fiouse, fuse (f)	*fusible*	fuse
fournaise (f)	*chaudière*	furnace
foyer naturel (m)	*foyer*	natural fireplace
frotter	*cirer, astiquer*	to wax, shine
gardienne (f)	*baby-sitter*	baby-sitter
garde-robe (m)	*placard, vestiaire*	clothes cupboard, closet
grand déménagement (m)	*déménagement fait au printemps*	spring moving (Quebec)
grand ménage (m)	*nettoyage fait au printemps*	spring cleaning, house cleaning
gréyer une maison	*monter une maison*	to equip a house
guenille (f)	*chiffon*	rag
gyprock (m)	*bois au plâtre*	gyprock
huile de charbon (f)	*pétrole*	coal oil
huile à chauffage, de chauffage	*mazout*	heating oil
huile crue, huile crute	*pétrole brut*	crude petroleum
huile à lampe	*pétrole lampant*	coal oil
laveuse; laveuse à vaisselle (f)	*machine à laver; lave-vaisselle*	washing machine; dishwasher
lessiveuse (automatique) (f)	*machine à laver*	(automatic) washing machine
lingerie (f)	*literie*	bedding
lit de camp (m)	*lit de sangue*	cot
lit continental	*grand lit*	continental bed
lit simple, lit double, lit trois-quarts	*lit à une place, à deux places . . .*	single, double bed, three-quarter bed
marchette (f)	*chariot*	walker (for baby)
masonite (m)	*bois pressé*	masonite
faire le ménage de qch	*nettoyer qch*	to clean up something
moulin (à coudre, à laver) (m)	*machine (à coudre, à laver)*	(sewing, washing) machine

Canada	France	
office (f)	*bureau, cabinet de travail*	office
panneau (de table) (m)	*abattant, rallonge*	leaf, board (of table)
patio (m)	*cour en carrelage*	patio
patte (f)	*pied*	leg (of table, etc.)
peinturer	*peindre*	to paint (walls, houses, etc.)
dépeinturer	*enlever la peinture*	to take off the paint
pièce d'ameublement (f)	*élément de mobilier*	piece of furniture
pin noueux (m)	*pin*	knotty pine
piqué (m)	*protège-matelas*	mattress-cover
plancher (m)	*étage*	floor, storey
plogue (f)	*fiche; prise de courant*	plug
porte d'en arrière (f)	*porte de service*	back door
porte d'en avant, de dehors	*porte d'entrée*	front door
porte grillée, de grille, de passe, de scrigne	*porte moustiquaire*	screen door
pouvoir (m)	*courant; puissance*	power, hydro; power (of machine)
portique (m)	*vestibule*	vestibule, front hall
prélart (m)	*linoléum*	linoleum
salle à dîner (f)	*salle à manger*	dining room
salle familiale	*salle de séjour*	family room
salle privée	*salon réservé*	private room (in hotel)
salle de réception	*salon*	reception room
salle de récréation	*salle de jeu*	recreation room
Société Centrale d'Hypothèques et de Logement (f)		Central Mortgage and Housing Corporation
sofa (m)	*divan*	sofa
solarium (m)	*pièce vitrée, ouverte au soleil*	solarium, sun porch
sortie (f)	*prise*	outlet (electrical), plug

22

Canada	France	
souitche (f)	*commutateur*	switch
store vénitien (m), toile vénitienne (f)	*jalousie*	Venetian blind
table de bout (f)	*petite table*	end table
table à café	*table de salon*	coffee table
table à cartes	*table de jeu*	card table
table à cocktail	*table*	cocktail table
table à extension	*table à rallonge*	extension table
tapette (f)	*tue-mouches*	fly swatter
tapis mur à mur (m)	*(tapis) moquette, tapis cloué*	wall to wall carpeting
tapisserie (f)	*papier-tenture*	wallpaper
terrazzo (f)	*plancher en ciment et en marbre*	terrazzo
tête d'oreiller (f)	*taie d'oreiller*	pillowcase
toilettes (f,pl)	*W.C.*	toilet
toutes dépenses payées	*charges comprises*	utilities included
trimer (un appartement, etc.)	*nettoyer et décorer*	to clean up and decorate
tuile (f)	*carreau*	tile (for wall or floor)
tuiler	*couvrir de "tuiles", de carreaux*	to tile
vidanges (f); vidanger	*ordures; enlever les ordures*	garbage; to clean up
vivoir (m)	*living, salon*	living room

Divers (Miscellaneous)

bas de porte (m)	*seuil*	threshold, doorstep
se bâtir, se construire	*se faire bâtir une maison*	to have a house built
baywindow, bow-window (m)	*fenêtre en saillie*	baywindow
bécosses (m,pl)	*latrines, cabinets*	backhouse, outhouse
brique à feu (f)	*brique réfractaire*	firebrick

Maison, Bâtiments (Home, Buildings)

Canada	France	
cabouse (f)	*cambuse, cabane*	shack
centre communautaire (m)	*centre de loisirs*	community centre
couche de flat (f)	*couche de fond*	undercoat
cour d'en arrière (f)	*cour*	backyard
dalle (eau de dalle) (f)	*gouttière (eau pluviale)*	eavestrough, (rain water)
entrée (f)	*passage*	driveway
escalier de derrière (m)	*escalier dérobé, de service*	back stairs
escalier en spirale	*escalier en colimaçon*	spiral staircase
fondations (f), solage (m)	*fondement*	foundation
galerie (f) (se bercer sur la galerie)	*véranda, balcon*	balcony, veranda (to rock on the balcony)
garage double (m)	*garage à deux places*	double garage
gazon (m)	*pelouse*	lawn
jour de lavage (m)	*jour de la lessive*	wash day
mitaine (f)	*temple protestant*	Protestant church, meeting house
moucherolle (f)	*attrape-mouches*	fly sticker
perron (m)	*petite véranda*	small veranda, front landing
paysagé, e	*(terrain) aménagé*	landscaped
références (f)	*attestation*	references (to get into an apt. etc.)
rocaille (f)	*jardin alpin*	rock garden
salon funéraire (m)	*maison des pompes funèbres*	funeral home, parlour
faire une saucette chez qn	*faire une courte visite*	to pay a short visit to s.o.
souffleuse (f)	*machine à souffler la neige*	snow blower
sur la rue	*dans la rue*	on the street
avoir de la visite	*recevoir des visiteurs*	to have company

Quincaillerie (Hardware)

Canada	France	
accessoires, attachements (m, pl)	*pièces amovibles*	attachments
affûter, gosser	*amenuiser*	to whittle, to taper
gossures (f,pl), moulée, ripe (f)	*copeaux*	shavings
avisse (f)	*vis*	screw
balayeuse (f), électrolux (m)	*aspirateur*	electric vacuum cleaner
barouette (f)	*brouette*	wheelbarrow
barrure (f)	*serrure; verrou*	lock; bolt
batterie (f)	*accumulateur, pile*	battery
bec, nozzle (m), pipe (f)	*lance*	nozzle
bérigne (m)	*coussinet, bille*	bearing
biberon, huilier (m)	*burette*	oil can
bobine (f)	*canette*	spool (of thread) (for a sewing machine)
bôlte (f)	*boulon*	bolt
bôlter	*boulonner*	to bolt
boucaut (de peinture) (m)	*pot*	can (of paint)
boyau (m), hose (f)	*tuyau d'arrosage*	(garden) hose
broc (m)	*fourche*	(four-pronged) fork
broche (f)	*fil de fer*	wire
broche piquante	*barbelé*	barbed wire
broche à foin	*fil de fer servant à lier le foin pressé*	baling wire
brocheuse, tackeuse (f)	*agrafeuse*	stapler
brocher, tacker	*agrafer*	to staple, to tack
(lumière) brûlée	*grillée*	burnt out (bulb)
castille (f)	*acier coulé*	cast steel
chaudière (f)	*seau (en métal)*	(metal) pail

Canada	France	
coppe (f)	*cuivre*	copper
(corde) extension (f)	*rallonge*	extension (cord)
couvert (m)	*couvercle*	cover, lid
crobarre (m, f)	*pince-monseigneur*	crowbar
cultivateur (à jardin) (m), bêcheuse (f)	*motoculteur*	rotor tiller
daille (m)	*filière*	die
drille (f), moine (m)	*foret, perceuse*	(electric) drill
échelle à extension (f)	*échelle à coulisse*	extension ladder
électrolier (m)	*lustre, plafonnier*	chandelier, ceiling light
épingle à couches (f)	*épingle de sûreté*	safety pin
éventail (m), fane (f)	*ventilateur*	house fan
fanal (m)	*lanterne, falot*	lantern
ferrée (f)	*bêche*	spade
ferronnerie (f), magasin de fer (m)	*quincaillerie*	hardware (store)
flashlight, lumière de poche (f)	*lampe de poche*	flashlight
fixtures (f)	*appareils d'éclairage*	fixtures
gaffe (f)	*dérivotte*	hook (gaff) used in logging
galon, guédge (m)	*ruban à mesurer*	tape measure
godendard (m)	*passe-partout*	cross-cut saw
gril (m)	*grille*	grill (of barbecue, etc.)
isolant (m)	*isolateur*	insulator
kit (m)	*jeu, trousse*	kit
lumière (f)	*ampoule*	(light) bulb
lumière d'extension, rallonge (f)	*baladeuse*	extension light
moppe(f)	*balai à franges, à laver*	mop
morceau (m), partie (f)	*pièce*	part (of machine)
moulin à tondre, moulin à gazon (m)	*tondeuse*	lawn mower
noix (f)	*écrou*	nut

Canada	France	
papier brun (m)	*papier gris, d'emballage*	brown paper
papier sablé	*papier de verre*	sandpaper
peindre	*peindre*	to paint (as an artist)
peinturer	*peindre*	to paint
picosseuse (f)	*bipenne*	(double-sided) axe
picosser	*utiliser une bipenne*	to use an axe
pied-de-roi (m)	*règle pliante; ruban*	carpenter's rule; measuring tape
pine (f)	*cheville, goupille*	pin (in apparatus)
planeur (m)	*rabot*	plane
planter un clou	*enfoncer*	to hammer a nail
pôle (m)	*tringle à rideaux*	curtain rod
polisseuse (f)	*cireuse, polissoir*	floor polisher
porte-ordures, porte-poussière (m)	*pelle à main, ramasse-poussière*	dustpan
prélart (m)	*linoléum*	linoleum, tile
ratchet (m)	*tournevis à cliquet*	ratchet (screwdriver)
receptacle (m)	*douille*	socket
ruban-cache, ruban à masquer (m)	*ruban*	masking tape
sablage (m)	*ponçage*	sanding (of floor, etc.)
sabler	*poncer*	to sand
sableuse, finisseuse (f)	*ponceuse*	electric sander
scrépeur (m)	*grattoir*	scraper
seau, siau (m)	*seau en bois*	wooden pail, bucket
shellac (m)	*laque, vernis*	shellac
shellaquer	*vernir*	to shellac
support (m)	*cintre; porte-(qch)*	coat hanger; rack (towel rack, etc.)
soudage (m)	*soudure*	solder; soldering, welding
taraud (m)	*écrou*	nut
tarauder	*visser*	to screw
détarauder	*dévisser*	to unscrew

Quincaillerie (Hardware)

Canada	France	
tépe (m)	*chatterton*	tape
téper	*chattertonner*	to tape
torche (f)	*lampe à essence; chalumeau*	oil lamp; blowtorch
tordeur (m)	*essoreuse*	wringer (of washing machine)
tournavis (m)	*tournevis*	screwdriver
tournavis Phillips	*tournevis à tête étoilée*	Phillips screwdriver
tournavis Robertson	*tournevis à tête carrée*	Robertson screwdriver
vadrouille (f)	*balai à franges; balayeuse*	mop; sweeper
vadrouiller	*balayer*	to mop; to sweep
virebrequin (m)	*vilebrequin*	brace and bit
wrench (m)	*clef*	wrench

Ville et Spectacles (City and Entertainment)

Canada	France	
admission (f)	*entrée*	admission
admission gratuite	*entrée libre*	free admission
barbotte (f)	*casino illicite*	illegal gambling joint
bloc (m), coin de rue (m)	*pâté de maisons*	block
boîte d'alarme (f)	*avertisseur d'incendie*	alarm box
boîte à chansons	*boîte pour les "chansonniers"*	coffee house
borne fontaine (f), hydrant (m)	*bouche d'incendie*	fire hydrant
cartoune (f), comique (m)	*dessin animé*	cartoon
chansonnier (m)	*interprète-compositeur*	song writer and singer
charrue (f)	*chasse-neige*	snow plow
ciné-parc, drive-in, théâtre en plein air (m)		drive-in theatre
club de nuit (m)	*boîte de nuit*	night club
collection, cueillette des vidanges (f)	*enlèvement des ordures*	garbage collection
déneigement (m)	*enlèvement de la neige*	snow removal
équipe des déneigeurs (f)	*ceux qui enlèvent la neige*	snow removal team
dompe (f)	*dépotoir*	dump
domper	*décharger*	to dump
jouer à guichets fermés	*faire salle comble*	to play to a full house
gratte (f)	*pelle*	snow plow, shovel
gratter	*déblayer*	to plow
grill (m)	*restaurant avec dancing*	bar and grill, night club

Canada	France	
lumière (f)	*feu*	traffic light
maison de paris (f)	*maison de jeux*	gambling house
maître de cérémonies (m)	*présentateur*	master of ceremonies
parc d'amusements (m)	*parc d'attractions*	amusement park
passage (m), traverse (f), (de pietons)	*passage clouté*	crosswalk
Place (Ville Marie, de Ville . . .) (f)	*centre commercial*	Downtown Centre, Mall
poste de pompiers (m), station de feu (f)	*poste d'incendie*	fire station
préviou, prévue (f)	*film annonce*	preview
rue commerciale (f)	*rue commerçante*	business street
rue transversale	*petite rue*	side street
salle de danse (f)	*dancing*	dance hall
salle de pool	*salle de billard*	pool hall
sloche, slotche, slush (f)	*gadoue*	slush
spectacle continuel (m)	*spectacle permanent*	continuous showing
station de gaz (f)	*poste d'essence*	gas station
station de police	*poste de police*	police station
stationnement (m)	*parking*	parking lot
taverne (f)	*brasserie*	tavern, beverage room, hotel
théâtre (m)	*cinéma*	movie theatre
trafic (m)	*circulation*	traffic
village (m)	*partie commerciale d'une ville*	downtown area
aller aux vues (f)	*aller au cinéma*	to go to the show, to the movies

Magasins et Commerce (Stores and Commerce)

Canada	France	
aubaine (f), barguine (m)	*occasion, bonne affaire*	bargain
barguiner	*marchander*	to bargain
barguinage (m)	*marchandage*	bargaining
bar laitier (m)	*crémerie*	dairy bar
bazar (m), vente du trottoir (f)	*solde en plein air, étalage*	sidewalk sale
binerie (f)	*petite épicerie; gargote*	small grocery store; greasy spoon
buanderie (f)	*blanchisserie*	laundry
buanderette (f)	*laverie automatique*	laundromat, coin laundry
centre d'achats (m)	*centre commercial*	shopping centre, shopping plaza
cinq-dix-quinze, quinze-cents (m)	*bazar, prisunic*	dime store, five-and-dime
Commission des liqueurs; Régie, Société des alcools (f)		Liquor Control Board
delicatessen (m)	*épicerie fine; restaurant avec charcuterie*	delicatessen
département (m)	*comptoir, rayon*	department
épicerie licenciée (f)	*épicerie*	licensed grocery
ferronnerie (f), magasin de fer (m)	*quincaillerie*	hardware store
fontaine (f)	*comptoir où on vend des boissons gazeuses*	soda fountain
grocerie (f)	*épicerie*	grocery (store)
magasin d'alimentation naturelle, d'alimentation santé (m)	*magasin de produits de régime*	health food store

31

Canada	France	
magasin de cadeaux et variétiés		gift and variety store
magasin du coin	*petit magasin*	corner store
magasin d'escompte	*magasin qui vend au rabais*	discount store
magasin général	*magasin qui vend un peu de tout*	general store
magasin de marchandises sèches	*mercerie*	dry goods store
magasin à rayons	*grand magasin*	department store
magasin de tabac, tabagie (f)	*bureau de tabac*	cigar store, news and smoke shop
magasin de tissus (à la verge)		yard goods store
magasinage (m)	*courses, shopping*	shopping
magasiner	*faire du shopping*	to go shopping
mail (m)	*rue commerçante fermée aux voitures*	mall
marché à viande (m)	*boucherie*	meat market
mercerie pour hommes (f)	*magasin de confection . . .*	men's clothing store
nettoyeurs (m)	*pressing*	cleaners
pas de dépôt	*pas de consigne*	no deposit
plaza (f)	*centre commercial*	plaza
rafle (f)	*déballage*	rummage sale
réduction (f)	*rabais*	reduction
de seconde main, usagé, e	*d'occasion*	second-hand, used
spécial, aux (m)	*objet à rabais*	special
stand de journaux (m)	*kiosque*	newsstand
valeur (f)	*économie*	value
vendeur (m)	*article qui se vend bien*	'good seller
vente (f)	*solde*	sale
vente de débarras, d'écoulement (m)	*vente de soldes*	clearance sale
vente de feu	*solde à la suite d'un incendie*	fire sale

Vêtements et Bijouterie (Clothing and Jewellery)

Canada	France	
accroc, raccroc (m)	*déchirure*	tear
ajustage (m)	*essayage*	fitting
altérations (f)	*modifications, retouches*	alterations
atriquage (f)	*accoutrement*	get-up, strange clothes
mal atriqué	*mal habillé*	poorly dressed
atriqué	*affublé*	dressed ridiculously
attacher (un manteau)	*boutonner, fermer*	to button up (a coat, etc.)
attelage (m)	*suspensoir*	athletic support
badge (f)	*plaque*	badge
barniques (f)	*lunettes*	glasses, specs
bas (m)	*chaussette*	sock
bas-culottes (m)	*collant*	panty hose
basques (f)	*revers*	lapels
bloomeurs (f)	*culotte bouffante*	bloomers
bobettes (f,pl), short, sous-vêtement (m)	*slip*	men's underwear (short)
bottine (f)	*botte*	laced, buckled boot
bottine de ski	*chaussure de ski*	ski boot
boucle (f)	*noeud papillon*	bow tie
boules à mites (f)	*boules de naphtaline*	moth balls
bourse, sacoche (f)	*sac à main*	purse
brassière (f)	*soutien-gorge*	brassiere
broche (à tricoter) (f)	*aiguille*	(knitting) needle
butin (m)	*effets usagés; vêtements*	old clothes; clothes

Vêtements et Bijouterie (Clothing and Jewellery)

Canada	France	
cache-oreilles (m), passe (f)	*sorte de bandeau en forme de casque à écouteurs pour protéger les oreilles du froid*	ear muffs
calotte (f)	*casquette*	cap
camisole (f), (petit) corps (m)	*maillot de corps*	undershirt
canot (m), claque (f)	*snowboot, caoutchouc*	toe rubber
capiche, capine, capuche (f)	*coiffure de femme avec gorgères*	bonnet, cape
capot (m)	*paletot*	overcoat
capot de chat	*pelisse en peau de raton laveur*	raccoon coat
casque (m)	*bonnet; casquette*	cap
casque de poil	*bonnet de fourrure*	fur hat
ceinture fléchée (f)	*ceinture chinée*	traditional French-Canadian belt or sash, arrow sash
change (m)	*rechange*	change of clothes
chausse (f)	*brodequin*	laced boot
chaussette (f)	*pantoufle*	slipper
chausson (m)	*chaussette de grosse laine*	heavy wool sock
bien checké	*bien habillé*	well-dressed, all dressed up
chienne, froque (f)	*sarrau*	smock
coat (m)	*blouson, manteau, veste*	coat, sports jacket
coco (m)	*chapeau melon*	bowler (hat)
col (m)	*cravate*	tie, necktie
collerette (m)	*mante, pèlerine*	woman's cape
collet (m)	*col*	collar
combinaison (f)	*caleçon long*	long underwear (one piece)
cordon (m)	*lacet*	shoelace
costume (m)	*uniforme*	uniform
costume de bain (m)	*maillot de bain*	bathing suit
coupe-vent (m)	*blouson*	windbreaker
C'est pas cousable.	*On ne peut pas le coudre.*	You can't sew it.

34

Canada	France	
crémone (f)	*cache-nez*	head-scarf
cuiller à soulier (f)	*chausse-pieds*	shoehorn
se décapoter	*enlever son manteau*	to take off one's coat
se déchanger	*se changer*	to change (clothes)
se dégreyer	*enlever son manteau, ses bottes, etc.*	to take off one's coat, boots, etc.
défilé de mode (m), parade de mode (f)	*présentation des collections*	fashion show
écourtichée	*habillée d'une robe très courte*	wearing a short dress
s'emmailloter	*s'habiller chaudement*	to dress warmly
empois (m)	*amidon*	starch
épingle à linge (f)	*fichoir*	clothes peg
épinglette (f)	*broche; épingle de cravate*	brooch; tie clip, tie pin
espadrilles (f), running-shoes (m), shoeclaques (f), souliers de course, souliers de gymnastique, souliers de sport, souliers de tennis, souliers de toile (m)	*tennis, baskets*	running shoes
flaille (f)	*braguette*	fly
forme de soulier (f)	*embauchoir*	shoetree
fril (m)	*jabot*	frill, ruffle
galoche (f)	*chaussure usée; couvre-chaussures*	used or out of shape shoe; overshoe
gilet (m)	*tout vêtement à manches; manteau, chandail*	any piece of clothing with sleeves; coat, sweater
grandeur (f)	*pointure (chaussures, chapeaux, gants), taille (habit, robe)*	size

Canada	France	
grappins (m)	*crampons*	spikes (for shoes), studs
se gréyer	*s'habiller*	to dress, get dressed
bien gréyé	*bien habillé*	well-dressed
habit, habillement (m)	*complet, costume*	suit
habit tout fait, sur mesure	*complet confection*	ready-made suit
habit à queue	*habit*	tailcoat
jaquette (f)	*chemise, robe de nuit*	nightgown
jaunir	*roussir*	to scorch (with iron)
jonc (m)	*alliance, bague*	wedding ring, engagement ring
jumpeur (m)	*sorte de jupe*	jumper
langue (f)	*languette*	tongue (of shoe)
large	*grand*	large (size)
linge (m)	*vêtements*	clothes
linge de corps	*sous-vêtements*	underwear
mackinaw, maquina (m)	*manteau de bûcheron*	lumberjack coat
médium	*moyen*	medium (size)
se mettre sur son 36, sur son 98	*se mettre sur son 31*	to dress up, put on one's Sunday best
mitaine (f)	*moufle*	mitt, mitten
noir à chaussures, poli (m)	*cirage, pâte*	shoe polish
pantalons (m), (une paire de pantalons)	*pantalon (sing)*	(a pair of) pants
pantalon court	*short*	shorts
pardessus (m)	*couvre-chaussures, bottes*	overshoes, boots
parka (m)	*anorak*	parka, winter coat
patch (f)	*pièce*	patch,
patcher	*rapiécer*	to patch
pend'oreilles (m)	*boucle d'oreille, pendant d'oreilles*	earring
petit balai (m)	*vergette, brosse à habit*	clothes brush
pichou (m)	*mocassin*	Indian moccasin

Canada	France	
être en pieds de bas	*être en chaussettes*	to be in one's stocking feet
point (m)	*pointure*	size (of shoe)
presser	*repasser*	to press
pressage (m)	*repassage*	pressing
être en queue de chemise	*être en pans de chemise*	to be in one's shirt-tails
raboudiner	*rafistoler*	to mend
raboudinage (m)	*rafistolage*	mending
refouler	*rétrécir*	to shrink
slaques (m)	*pantalon (de sport)*	slacks
slip (m), slippe (f)	*combinaison-jupon*	woman's slip
snap (m)	*bouton-pression*	snap
soulier (m)	*chaussure*	shoe
stud (m)	*bouton de manchette*	cuff link
support (m)	*cintre*	(clothes) hanger
swell	*chic*	fashionable, snazzy
taille d'une robe (f)	*corsage*	body, bodice of dress
taponner	*friper*	to crease, wrinkle
tournaline (f)	*béret*	beret
trousseau (de bébé) (m)	*layette*	set of baby garments, layette
tuque (f)	*bonnet de laine*	tuque
tuxedo (m)	*smoking*	tuxedo
usé au coton	*usé jusqu'à la corde*	worn to the thread
veste (f)	*gilet*	vest
veste de cuir	*blouson de cuir*	leather jacket
veston (m)	*veste*	dress jacket, sports jacket
vêtements de base (m)	*sous-vêtements*	lingerie, underclothing
zippe, zippeur (m)	*fermeture éclair*	zipper
zipper (dézipper)	*fermer (ouvrir)*	to zip up (to unzip)
se zipper (se dézipper)	*fermer (ouvrir) sa fermeture éclair*	to pull up (to pull down) one's zipper

Tissus et Couleurs (Fabrics and Colours)

Canada	France	
absorbant, e (coton absorbant, etc.)	*hydrophile*	absorbent
barré, e	*rayé, à rayures*	striped
burlap (m)	*toile d'emballage*	burlap
carreauté, e	*à carreaux*	checked
corderoi (m)	*velours côtelé*	corduroy
coton à fromage (m)	*étamine*	cheese cloth
coton jaune	*coton écru*	raw cotton
cuir patente (m)	*verni*	patent leather
cuirette (f)	*similicuir*	artificial leather
s'échiffer	*s'effilocher*	to ravel, fray
étoffe du pays (f)	*drap de laine épais tissé à la maison*	homespun
étoffe (f)	*morceau d'étoffe*	piece of material
flanellette (f)	*finette*	flannelette
guenille (f)	*chiffon*	rag
kid (m)	*chevreau*	kid (leather)
matériel (m)	*étoffe*	material
motton (m)	*noeud*	knot (in a fabric)
satine (f)	*satinette*	satinette
stretchy	*extensible*	stretchy

Couleurs

bleu marin	*bleu marine*	navy blue
brun	*marron*	brown (shoes, etc.)
drabe	*beige*	beige
marron	*lie de vin*	maroon

L'Amour (Love)

Canada	France	
s'accoter	*commencer à vivre en concubinage*	to start living together, shack up
accoté, e	*qui vit en concubinage, amant, maîtresse*	lover, mistress, common law husband or wife
vivre accotés	*vivre en concubinage*	to live together
agace-pissette (f)	*aiguicheuse, allumeuse*	tease, cockteaser
aller voir les filles	*courtiser les jeunes filles*	to go out with girls
ami de garçon, boy-friend, cavalier, chum, tchomme (m)	*(petit) ami, futur, soupirant*	boyfriend
amie de fille, blonde, fille, girl-friend, petite mère (f)	*(petite) amie, future*	girlfriend
(se) faire ami avec qn	*se lier d'amitié avec qn*	to make friends with s.o.
être en amour avec qn	*être amoureux de qn*	to be in love
tomber en amour avec qn	*tomber amoureux de qn*	to fall in love
faire manger de l'avoine à qn	*supplanter qn comme amoureux*	to steal s.o.'s girl
faire gratter qn	*couper l'herbe sous les pieds de qn*	to cut s.o.'s grass
baiser	*embrasser*	to kiss
bec (m)	*baiser, bécot*	kiss, peck
vieux boque, vieux buck (m)	*vert galant*	elderly lady-killer, gay dog
botte (f)	*action de faire l'amour*	lay, screw
être une bonne botte	*bien faire l'amour*	to be a good lay

L'Amour (Love)

Canada	France	
prendre une botte	*faire l'amour*	to get laid
bras cassé, fif, fifi (m)	*homosexuel, tapette, pédé*	homosexual, queer
casser	*rompre*	to break up, separate
chanter la pomme (à une fille)	*conter fleurette*	to talk up, hustle (a girl)
cousinage (m)	*amour entre cousins*	love between cousins
se crosser	*se masturber*	to masturbate, to jack off
date, déte (f)	*rendez-vous*	date
déviarger (une fille), faire sauter la cerise	*dépuceler, déniaiser*	to deflower, take (a girl's) virginity, cop her cherry
s'engager	*se fiancer*	to get engaged
farauder qn, fréquenter qn	*faire la cour à qn*	to go out with s.o.
fréquentations (f, pl)	*action de sortir régulièrement*	steady dating
fourrer qn, se mettre	*baiser qn*	to lay, screw
fringalet (m)	*coureur discret*	old fox, a man who has the occasional affair
galanter	*flatter*	to flatter
perdre sa josepheté	*perdre sa virginité*	to lose one's virginity
avoir le kick sur qn, être stoqué sur qn	*avoir le béguin pour qn, être toqué de qn*	to have a crush on s.o.
loup, maquereau (m)	*coureur, séducteur*	wolf
marcou (m)	*entreteneur*	lover, keeper
marier qn	*épouser qn*	to marry s.o.
pas marieux	*qui ne montre aucun goût de se marier, célibataire endurci*	not the marrying kind, confirmed bachelor
faire du necking	*s'embrasser passionnément*	to neck, to French kiss
faire du parking	*se peloter dans une voiture et dans un endroit isolé*	to park

Canada	France	
dénicher des parkings	*espionner ceux qui font du "parking"*	to go bumper jumping
pelote, plotte (f)	*prostituée; femme légère*	prostitute; easy woman
pimp (m)	*entremetteur*	pimp
poignasser qn	*peloter qn*	to pet s.o., to neck with s.o.
se poigner	*se peloter*	to pet
sauteux de clôtures (m)	*don Juan*	womanizer
sexé, e	*sexy*	sexy
sortir steady	*se voir régulièrement*	to go steady
sucette (f)	*suçon*	hickey
suivant (m)	*garçon d'honneur*	best man
suivante (f)	*fille d'honneur*	maid of honour
connaître le tabac	*s'y connaître, n'être pas né d'hier*	to have experience, to have been around
tomber dans l'oeil de qn	*taper dans l'oeil de qn*	to catch s.o.'s eye, to attract s.o.
tripoteux (m)	*peloteur*	cuddler, s.o. with Roman hands
trotter	*courailler*	to run around, chase after the opposite sex
être trotteuse	*être un peu coureuse*	to be boy crazy, be a flirt

Corps et Maladies (Body and Diseases)

Canada	France	
acheter un enfant	*accoucher d'un enfant*	to have a baby
être affligé du coeur, être pris du coeur	*malade du coeur*	to have a bad heart
apitchouner, atchoumer	*éternuer*	to sneeze
arupiaux (m), mopses (f), orupiaux (m)	*oreillons*	mumps
baboune (f)	*grosse lèvre*	thick lip
bajotte (f)	*joue, bajoue, grosse joue*	fat cheek
ballant (m)	*équilibre*	balance
être en balloune, être pleine	*être enceinte*	to be pregnant
baquais, baquet (m), baquaise (f)	*personne grosse et courte*	short, stocky person
être baquaise	*être obèse*	to be fat
barre du cou (f)	*os du cou, nuque*	neck bone
bégayeux, euse; bégueux, euse	*bègue*	stutterer
bizoune, graine, pissette (f)	*pénis, verge*	penis, tool
bloc (m), bolle (f), casque, coco (m)	*boule, tête*	head, noggin
boules (f), cenels (m), chnolles, gosses (f), snels (m)	*couilles, testicules*	balls, testicles
bouscaud (m)	*homme trapu et costaud*	stocky, hefty person
être rendu au boutte	*être à bout*	to be dead tired
avoir les bronches	*avoir une bronchite*	to have bronchitis
calé, e	*chauve*	bald

Canada	France	
caler	*devenir chauve*	to go bald
califourchon (m)	*derrière*	backside, bottom
canne (f)	*jambe*	leg, gam
charrier, avoir le corps lâche, avoir le flou, avoir mal au ventre, avoir le va-vite	*avoir la diarrhée*	to have diarrhea, the runs, a stomach ache
check-up (m)	*examen général*	checkup
chromo (m)	*personne laide*	wipe-out, ugly person
se clairer d'une maladie	*guérir . . .*	to get over a disease
condition physique (f)	*forme physique*	physical condition
consomption (f)	*tuberculose*	consumption, T.B.
coq-l'oeil (m)	*bigle, loucheur; borgne*	cross-eyed person; one-eyed person
couette (f)	*mèche, tresse*	braids, pigtails
courte-haleine (f)	*essoufflement*	shortness of breath
créature (f)	*femme*	female, woman
se crever	*contracter une hernie*	to rupture oneself
avoir les yeux croches	*être bigle*	to be cross-eyed
cute	*mignon*	cute
dalot (m)	*dalle, gosier*	throat
débattre (Le coeur me débat.), toquer (J'ai le coeur qui toque.)	*battre*	to beat (heart) (My heart is pounding.)
se dégripper	*se guérir de la grippe*	to come out of the flu
déguiser	*défigurer, enlaidir*	to spoil the appearance (of s.o.)
Mon bras me démanche.	*. . . démange.*	My arm is itchy.
mal denté, e; mal dentelé, e	*mal endenté*	a person who has bad teeth
dérangé, e; troublé, e	*faible d'esprit*	disturbed (in the mind)
détorse (f)	*entorse*	sprain

Canada	France	
avoir le pied détors	*avoir une entorse au pied*	to have a sprained ankle
se dôper, se dôser	*se droguer*	to take drugs
dôpé (m)	*narcomane*	addict, dope fiend
dose (f)	*maladie vénérienne*	case of V.D., dose
échappe, écharpe (f)	*écharde*	sliver
s'éjarrer	*perdre pied*	to lose one's footing
égossé	*châtré*	castrated
s'estropier	*se blesser*	to hurt oneself
avoir de la façon	*avoir l'air heureux*	to look happy
falle (f)	*poitrine, gorge*	chest, throat
avoir la falle basse	*avoir faim*	to be hungry
partir (être) en famille	*devenir (être) enceinte*	to get (be) pregnant, in a family way
feu sauvage (m)	*herpès*	cold sore
avoir les (grandes) fièvres	*avoir la fièvre typhoïde*	to have typhoid fever
Ça file bien.	*Je me sens bien.*	I feel all right.
Il ne file pas.	*Il ne se sent pas bien.*	He's not feeling so good.
foufounes (f)	*derrière*	rear end, cheeks
fourche, raie (f)	*entre-jambes*	crotch
fraise (f) (Je n'aime pas sa fraise.)	*Il a une sale gueule*	face (I don't like his looks.)
gadille, guédille (f)	*roupie, morve*	mucus, snot
gala, gale (f)	*croûte, eschare*	scab
geler	*insensibiliser*	to freeze (tooth)
gorgoton (m)	*pomme d'Adam, gorge*	Adam's apple, throat
grafigner	*égratigner*	to scratch, graze
grafignure (f)	*égratignure*	scratch
griller	*bronzer*	to tan
griser	*grisonner*	to turn gray
s'infliger une blessure	*se blesser*	to get injured

Canada	**France**	
irrégularité (f)	*constipation*	irregularity, constipation
jack (m)	*personne très grande*	tall person
jos (m)	*seins*	breasts
loucheux, euse	*loucheur*	cross-eyed
être malade	*être indisposée*	to be having a period
malade au lit	*cloué au lit*	sick in bed
mal-en-train	*indisposé, souffrant*	out of sorts, not feeling well
se manger	*se gratter*	to scratch oneself
matière (f)	*pus*	pus
matiérer	*suppurer*	to ooze pus
matiéreux, euse	*suppurant*	full of pus
mature	*mûr*	mature
mordée (f)	*morsure*	bite
se morfondre	*s'épuiser*	to get tired out
morfondant, e	*épuisant*	exhausting
mosselles (f)	*biceps*	(arm) muscles
mouche de moutarde (f)	*sinapisme*	mustard plaster
palotte	*maladroit*	clumsy
pantoufle, pelote, plotte (f)	*vagin*	vagina, pussy
pas d'allure (m)	*gauche, maladroit*	clumsy person
avoir la tête comme une patinoire	*être chauve comme un oeuf*	to be as bald as a billiard ball
peaux mortes (f)	*pellicules*	dandruff
avoir du pep	*avoir de l'énergie*	to have pep
peppé, e	*énergique*	peppy
un beau pétard	*une femme bien bâtie*	a well-stacked woman
grosse picote (f)	*variole, petite vérole*	smallpox
picote noire	*variole hémorragique*	smallpox

Canada	France	
picote volante	*varicelle*	chickenpox
picoté, e	*grêlé*	pockmarked
pivelé, e	*taché de rousseur*	freckled
fille bien plantée	*. . . bien faite*	well-built girl
pleumer	*perdre ses cheveux*	to lose one's hair
poque (f)	*bleu, bosse*	bruise, bump
poitrail (m)	*poitrine énorme*	large chest
poutine (une grosse poutine)	*personne grasse*	fat person
prendre la fraîche	*prendre froid*	to catch a chill
rapporté, e (dent, cheveux)	*faux*	false (teeth, hair)
raqué, e	*épuisé*	tired out
rayons X (m)	*radiographie*	X rays
recopié (C'est ton frère tout recopié.)	*ressemblant*	identical (He's the spitting image of your brother.)
réhabilitation (f)	*réadaptation*	rehabilitation
respir (m)	*respiration; souffle; soupir*	breathing; breath; sigh
resté, e	*épuisé*	tired out
restituer	*vomir*	to bring up, vomit
rifle (m)	*eczéma, exanthème*	eczema, rash
rognon (m)	*rein*	kidney
rousselé, e	*qui a des taches de rousseur*	freckled
rousseler	*se couvrir de taches de rousseur*	to freckle
rousselures (f)	*taches de rousseur*	freckles
roteux, euse	*roteur*	person who burps
saloperie (f)	*escarbille, poussière*	cinder, dust, speck (in the eye)
savaté, e	*fatigué*	tired out
séparation, séparure (f)	*raie*	part (in hair)
sexé, e	*sexy*	sexy
siler (Les oreilles me silent, etc.)	*gémir; tinter; siffler*	to cry; to tingle, buzz; to wheeze
sileux, euse	*qui "sile"*	buzzing; wheezing

Canada	France	
slaque	*efflanqué*	loose-limbed
un grand slaque	*homme grand et efflanqué*	tall and loose-limbed man
sueux, euse	*qui transpire beaucoup*	sweaty
tomber d'un mal	*souffrir d'épilepsie*	to suffer from epilepsy, to have fits
se torcher	*nettoyer son derrière*	to wipe one's rear, oneself
toutoune	*grassouillette*	plump
vanné, e	*épuisé*	exhausted
se vider	*s'évacuer*	to have a bowel movement

Pharmacie, Produits de Beauté (Drug Store, Beauty Products)

Canada	France	
bandage, bandaid, diachylon, pansement, plasteur (m)	*tricostéril*	bandaid
barre de savon (f)	*pain de savon*	bar of soap
bobettes, bobépines, broches, pinces, pincettes (à cheveux) (f)	*épingles*	bobby pins
faire de la broue	*mousser*	to foam
compact (m)	*poudrier*	compact
conditionneur à cheveux (m)	*lotion*	hair conditioner
crème, huile (pour les cheveux) (f), fixatif (m)	*brillantine*	hair cream, hair oil
crème de rinçage, rince-crème (f)	*lotion après rinçage*	cream rinse
crème à barbe (f)	*mousse à raser*	shaving cream
cutex, poli (à ongles) (m)	*vernis à ongles*	nail polish
débarbouillette (f)	*gant de toilette*	face-cloth
diachylon, ruban adhésif (m)	*sparadrap*	adhesive tape
égaliser, tailler, trimer	*rafraîchir*	to trim
fixatif aérosol, laqueur, spray, spray net, vaporisant (m)	*laque, fixateur*	hair spray
kleenex, papier-mouchoir, tissu (m)	*mouchoir en papier*	kleenex
lotion après rasage, avant rasage (f)	*after-shave, lotion*	after-shave, pre-shave (lotion)
mascara (m)	*maquillage (pour les cils)*	mascara

Canada	France	
médicamenté, e	*médicamenteux*	medicated
ondulation (f), permanent (m)	*modeling, permanente*	permanent
papier de toilette (m)	*papier hygiénique*	toilet paper
pâte dentrifrice, à dents (f)	*dentifrice*	toothpaste
peignure (f)	*coiffure*	hairdo
prescription (f)	*ordonnance*	prescription
remplir une prescription	*exécuter une ordonnance*	to fill a prescription
rasoir droit (m)	*rasoir à main*	straight razor
se renipper	*faire sa toilette*	to wash, shave, etc.
rimmel (m)	*maquillage (pour les paupières)*	makeup, eye shadow
rince-bouche (m)	*eau dentifrice*	mouthwash
savon de castille (m)	*savon de Marseille*	yellow soap
savon de toilette	*savonnette*	toilet soap
savonnette (f)	*blaireau*	shaving brush
savonnier (m)	*porte-savon*	soap tray, dish
savonnure (f)	*mousse de savon*	soap suds
shampou (m)	*shampooing*	shampoo
tablette (f)	*comprimé*	pill, tablet
vitaminisé, e	*vitaminé*	vitaminized

Le Temps (The Weather)

Canada	France	
abatage de pluie (m)	*rafale de pluie*	cloudburst
s'amollir	*s'adoucir*	to get milder
barre du jour (f)	*aube*	dawn, daybreak
Il pleut à boire debout.	*. . . à seaux*	It's pouring.
	. . . à verse	It's raining cats and dogs.
bordée de neige (f)	*forte tombée de neige*	heavy snowfall
à la brunante	*au crépuscule, à la nuit tombante*	at dusk, at nightfall
chute de neige (f)	*tombée de neige*	snowfall
clair d'étoiles (m)	*clarté des étoiles*	starlight
se clairer	*s'éclaircir*	to clear up
temps de cochon (m)	*temps de chien*	dirty weather
cru	*froid et humide*	raw
crudité (f)	*humidité froide*	raw weather
doux-temps (m)	*temps relativement doux suivant un grand froid*	milder weather, mild spell
il éclaire	*il fait des éclairs*	it's lightning
été des Indiens, été des sauvages (m)	*été de la Saint-Martin*	Indian summer
fret, frette	*froid*	cold
fret noir, fret sec (m)	*froid sibérien*	freezing cold
gelasser	*geler légerèment*	to be just freezing
grêlasser	*grêler légerèment*	to be hailing a bit
se morpionner	*se mettre au mauvais*	to get worse
mouillasser	*crachiner*	to be spitting, drizzling
mouillasseux, mouilleux	*pluvieux*	rainy
mouiller	*pleuvoir*	to be raining
neiges (f,pl)	*saison des neiges*	wintertime

Canada	France	
neigeasser	*neiger légèrement*	to be snowing a bit
noirceur (f)	*obscurité*	dark
poudrer	*voler en tourbillonnant*	to swirl (snow)
poudrerie (f)	*tempête de neige poudreuse, neige poudreuse balayée par le vent*	snowstorm, blowing snow (powdery snow)
rafaler	*souffler par rafales*	to gust (wind, snow)
sorcière, tourniquette (f)	*petite tornade*	twister
sucres (m,pl), temps des sucres (m)	*période du printemps où on fabrique le sucre d'érable*	maple syrup time
température (f)	*temps*	weather
une belle température	*un beau temps*	good, nice weather
venter	*faire du vent*	to be windy
pluie verglaçante	*pluie qui produit du verglas*	freezing rain

Géographie (Geography)

Divers (Miscellaneous)

Canada	France	
Anglais, e	*Canadien anglais*	English Canadian
Anglais d'Angleterre	*Anglais*	the English
barachois (m)	*petit port naturel*	small natural harbour
le bas de la paroisse	*partie est de la paroisse*	eastern part of the "parish"
Basse Ville (f) (Ottawa, Québec, etc.)		Lower Town
bayou (m)	*marécage*	bayou, swamp
bloke, British (m)	*Canadien anglais*	English Canadian (often pejorative)
bord (m)	*côté*	side (of street)
cousins, gens de l'autre bord	*Européens*	people from across the pond, Europeans (esp. the French)
de bord en bord (du Canada)	*d'un bout a l'autre du Canada*	from one end (of the country) to the other
bout, boutte (m)	*endroit, quartier*	area, district, place
dans le boutte	*dans les parages*	around here
Cajun (m)	*Acadien de la Louisiane*	Cajun
Canadien, ienne	*Canadien français*	French Canadian
Canayen	*Canadien français*	French Canadian (often pejorative)
canton (m), commune (f)		township
cantons de l'Est (m), Estrie (f)		Eastern Townships
Estrien, ienne		person from the Eastern Townships
carré (m)	*square*	square

Canada	France	
Chiac, acque		person from Moncton, Shediac
Cité de Montréal, etc.	*Ville de . . .*	City of Montreal etc.
comté (m)		county
concessions (f,pl)	*arrière-pays*	back country
d'une côte à l'autre	*d'un océan à l'autre*	from coast to coast
Côte Nord		North Shore
Côte du Pacifique		Pacific Coast
Côte Sud		South Shore
crique (f)	*ruisseau*	creek
dans l'Europe, dans le Québec	*en Europe, au Québec*	to, in Europe, to, in Quebec
descendre	*aller dans la direction du St-Laurent; aller*	to go down (to Montreal, etc.)
à drette	*à droite*	to the right
les Etats (m)	*Etats-Unis*	The States
étatsunien, ienne	*des Etats-Unis*	American
Le Fleuve	*le St-Laurent*	St. Lawrence River
Bas du fleuve (m)		Lower St. Lawrence
Français de France (m)	*Français*	French from France
Franco (m)	*Franco-Canadien*	French Canadian
Franco-Albertain, -Américain, -Manitobain, -Ontarien, etc.		French Albertan, American, Manitoban, Ontarian, etc.
Gaspésie (f)		Gaspé Peninsula
Gaspésien, ienne		person from the Gaspé
habitant (m)	*colon; fermier*	French settler; farmer, habitant
le haut de la paroisse	*partie ouest de la paroisse*	western part of the "parish"
le haut du village	*partie du village au-dessus de l'église par rapport au fleuve*	upper part of the village
en haut de Trois-Rivières	*en amont de . . .*	above, west of Three Rivers

Canada	France	
Haute Ville (f)		Upper Town
icitte	*ici*	here
Laurentides (f) (laurentien, ienne)		Laurentians (Laurentian)
Laurentie (f) (laurentien, ienne)	*le Québec, region du St-Laurent*	Quebec, St. Lawrence area (Laurentian)
les lignes (f)	*frontière américaine*	the border, the line
limite à bois (f)	*concession forestière*	lumber concession
localité (f)	*endroit*	locality
Royaume du Madawaska (m)		Northern New Brunswick
Madelinot, ote		Magdalen Islander
Malbaie (f)		Murray Bay
être sur la mappe	*être assez important (pour figurer sur la carte)*	to be on the map
Maskoutain, e		person from St. Hyacinthe
Mauricie (f) (Mauricien, ienne)		St. Maurice Valley (person from this area)
Métis, isse	*Métis de l'Ouest*	Métis
monter	*aller à l'inverse du cours du St-Laurent; aller*	to go up (to Montreal, etc.)
Néo-Canadien, ienne	*nouveau Canadien*	New Canadian
Néo-Ecossais, e		Nova Scotian
le Nord-Ouest (québécois)		North-Western Quebec
Nouvel Ontario, Nouveau Québec		Northern Ontario, Northern Quebec
Outaouais (m), Vallée de l'Outaouais (f)		Ottawa Valley
Outaouais, e		Ottawan
parc national, provincial (m)		national, provincial park
paroisse (f)	*municipalité rurale*	parish (rural municipality)

Canada	France	
pays d'en haut (m)	*région située au nord de Montréal, le Nord*	area north of Montreal, the North
piquer un travers	*prendre un raccourci*	to take a short cut
place (Quelle belle place!)	*endroit, ville*	place (What a beautiful place!)
planche	*plat*	flat (land, etc.)
presqu'américain, e		term used to describe the French-Canadian society
quartier latin (m)	*quartier latin de Québec*	Latin Quarter (university area in old Quebec City)
québécitude (f)		term used to describe the Quebec society
réserve (f)	*territoire réservé aux Indiens*	(Indian) reserve
rigolet (m)	*petit ruisseau*	small stream
Rocheuses (f)		Rockies
Royaume du Saguenay (Saguenéen, enne)		Kingdom of the Saguenay (person from the Saguenay)
Ste-Catherine est, ouest		St. Catherine East, West
Terre-Neuvien, ienne		Newfoundlander
tête carrée (f)	*Canadien anglais*	English Canadian (pejorative)
Trifluvien, ienne		person from Three Rivers
la vieille capitale	*Québec*	Quebec City
le vieux Montréal		Old Montreal
le Vieux-Pays (m)	*la France*	the Old Country
les Vieux-Pays	*l'Europe*	Europe
la Ville Reine	*Toronto*	Queen City (Toronto)
Voie maritime du St-Laurent (f)		St. Lawrence Seaway

Routes (Roads)

Canada	France	
C'est pas allable.	*C'est pas praticable.*	You can't get through.
Arrêt	*Stop*	Stop (sign)
balise (f)	*indicateur*	roadside indicator
Cédez	*Priorité*	Yield
chemin (m) (Chemin de la Côte des Neiges)	*boulevard*	road
chemin du roi	*route nationale*	King's highway; e.g. Highway 2 from Montreal to Quebec
chemin en corderoi	*chemin fait de billes*	corduroy road
côltar (m)	*goudron*	tar
côte (f)	*rue*	road, street (not necessarily sloped)
croche (m)	*virage*	turn
faire un croche	*faire un détour*	to make a detour
débloquer une route	*déblayer . . .*	to clear a road
descente (f)	*rue*	hill, road
détour (m)	*déviation; virage*	detour; turn
échangeur (m)	*bretelle*	interchange
fourche (f)	*bifurcation*	fork (in road)
(route de) gravelle, gravier, gravois (f)	*route de terre*	gravel road
impassable; passable	*impraticable; praticable*	impassable; passable (road)
jetée (f)	*route qui relie une île à la côte*	causeway
la Main, la Méne	*grand-rue*	the Main (St. Lawrence Blvd. in Montreal), any main street
montée (f)	*rue*	road, hill
pesée publique, pesée routière (f)	*balance*	weigh scales
planche à laver, roulière (f)	*route cahoteuse*	washboard (road)
ponté, e	*pavé en bois*	log-paved (bridge, etc.)

Canada	France	
se raccourcir	*prendre un raccourci*	to take a short cut
raccroc (m)	*virage*	turn, sharp curve
rang (m)	*chemin de campagne*	concession, line
(route) transcanadienne (f)		Trans Canada Highway
route transversale		side road
rue principale (f)	*grand-rue*	main street
ruelle (f)	*rue de service, petite rue*	service road, back street, alley
habiter sur la rue …	*habiter dans la rue …*	to live on … Street
traînant, e (route, chemin) …	*d'hiver*	sleigh (path, road)
traverse d'animaux (f)	*passage d'animaux*	cattle, deer crossing

Nature

Canada	France	
aboiteau (m)	*aboteau*	type of dam
batture (f)	*estran*	strand; rocky shore
billot (m)	*bille*	log
bois de grève, de marée (m), échourie (f)	*épave*	driftwood
boisé (m)	*terrain boisé*	wooded area, woodlot
bordages (m,pl)	*glaces adhérentes aux rives*	ice on bank of river
bouette(f)	*neige fondante*	wet snow
bouscueil (m)	*glaces mouvantes sur l'eau*	ice-floe
chaussée (de castors) (f)	*petit barrage*	(beaver) dam
clairons (m,pl)	*aurore boréale*	northern lights
coloniser la terre	*défricher et peupler la terre*	to clear and settle the land
corps-mort (m)	*tronc décomposé*	rotten stump
coulée (f)	*ravin, vallée*	ravine, valley
cran (m); crans (m,pl)	*rocher à fleur du sol; falaise*	flat rock; cliff
désert, essart (m)	*clairière*	clearing
eaux vives (f,pl)	*courant rapide*	swift current
écorre (f)	*rive escarpée*	steep river bank
falaise (f)	*escarpement*	bluff, escarpment
fondrière de mousse, fondrière moussue (f)	*muskeg*	muskeg
garnotte, grenotte (f)	*cailloux*	small stones
gazon de neige (m)	*neige découpée à la pelle*	blocks of shovelled snow
grain (m)	*fil*	grain (of wood)
gravelle (f), gravois (m)	*gravier*	gravel

Canada	France	
grignon (m)	*glace ou terre gelées*	lump of frozen earth or ice
jamme, prise (de billots) (f)	*embâcle*	log jam
passe (f)	*col*	pass, saddle (in mountains)
paysager	*aménager le paysage*	to landscape
pelotant, e	*qui fait de bonnes pelotes*	good packing (snow)
pigras (m)	*boue, bourbier*	mud
pigrasser	*patauger dans la boue*	to play in the mud
pigrasseux, euse	*plein de boue*	muddy
pulpe (f)	*pâte à papier*	pulp
rasé (m)	*clairière*	clearing in the woods
renouveau (m)	*nouvelle lune*	new moon
ripe (f)	*copeaux*	kindling, shavings
roche (f)	*caillou*	stone, small rock
savane (f)	*marécage; plaine*	swamp; treeless plain
terre en bois debout (f)	*terre boisée*	bush, forest area
tondre (m)	*amadou*	tinder (wood)
tondreux, euse	*desséché et poreux*	dry and porous (wood)

La Ferme (The Farm)

Canada	France	
abatis (m)	*terre défrichée mais non cultivée*	cleared but unworked land
alfalfa (f)	*luzerne*	alfalfa
anneuillère	*(vache) qui n'a pas eu de veau dans l'année*	dry (cow)
arrache-patates (m)	*arracheuse de pommes de terre*	potato picker
arrache-pierres (m)	*arracheuse de pierres*	stone puller
arrache-souche (m), essoucheuse (f)	*machine à arracher les souches*	stump puller
arranger	*châtrer*	to cut, fix (pigs, etc.)
attelage (m)	*harnais*	harness
barrure (f)	*stalle*	stall
batterie (f)	*aire*	(barn) floor
béle (f)	*balle (de foin)*	bale
béleur (m)	*presse*	baler
bonhomme (m)	*épouvantail*	scarecrow
bottine (f)	*gerbe*	sheaf
faire boucherie	*abattre un animal chez soi*	to butcher
bouettasser	*donner à manger*	to slop, feed
bouette (f)	*mangeaille, pâtée*	slop (chop mixed with water)
faire bouillir	*faire bouillir la sève d'érable*	to boil (the sap)
cabane à sucre (f)	*maisonnette où se fait le sirop d'érable*	(sugar) shanty
chouler, kisser, souquer (un chien contre . . .)	*exciter*	to sic (a dog on . . .)
circuit (m)	*terrain éloigné de la ferme*	back forty

Canada	France	
clairer	*défricher*	to clear (land)
clos de pacage (m)	*pâturage, pré*	pasture field
clôture de ligne (f)	*clôture séparant une ferme d'une autre*	line fence
combine (f)	*moissonneuse-batteuse*	combine
coulée (f)	*quantité de sève d'érable récoltée*	run (of sap)
dompter (un cheval)	*rompre, dresser*	to break in (a horse)
faire une donaison	*donner sa ferme à un fils*	to hand over the farm (to a son)
eau d'érable (f)	*sève d'érable*	sap
entailler	*faire une entaille à un érable, mettre une érablière en exploitation*	to tap
fourragère (f)	*machine qui fauche, hache et souffle les plantes d'ensilage*	forage harvester
grabeur (m)	*herse*	harrows
grainerie (f)	*grenier à blé*	granary
gratter les vaches	*nettoyer l'écurie*	to clean the stables
mettre en hivernement	*rentrer pour l'hiver*	to bring in for the winter (stock)
montée (f)	*chemin traversant une ferme*	lane
moulée (f)	*mouture*	chop, feed
moulin à battre (m)	*batteuse*	threshing machine
moulin à faucher	*faucheuse*	(hay) mower
mulon (m), vailloche (f)	*meulon, veillotte*	(hay, straw) stack
paire (m)	*pis*	(cow's) teat
râcler	*râteler*	to rake (hay)
rallonge (f)	*annexe (d'une grange)*	lean, extra bent, addition (to a barn)
semeuse (f)	*semoir*	seed drill
séparateur (m)	*écrémeuse*	separator
spanne, team (f)	*attelage*	team

La Ferme (The Farm)

Canada	**France**	
stouque (m)	*moyette*	stook
stouquer	*faire des moyettes*	to stook
sur une ferme	*dans une ferme*	on a farm
tasserie (f)	*fenil, grenier*	mow
taure (f)	*génisse*	heifer
faire de la terre	*défricher le sol*	to clear the land
tirer les vaches	*traire les vaches*	to milk the cows
tocson, onne	*décorné*	polled (cattle), mooley
trailer, tréleur (m), waguine (f)	*wagon de ferme*	wagon
faire le train	*soigner les animaux*	to do the chores
voyage (de foin, etc.) (m)	*chargement, charretée*	load (of hay, etc.)

Voyages et Moyens de Transport (Travel and Means of Transportation)

Canada	France	
acheter un billet	*prendre un billet*	to buy a ticket
auto (m,f), char (m), machine (f)	*voiture*	car
autobus (m)	*autocar, car*	bus (for highway travel)
auto-neige, moto-neige (f), skidoo (m)	*scooter des neiges*	snowmobile
banneau (m)	*traîneau à bascule*	dump sleigh
barlot, berlot (m)	*traîneau attelé*	box sleigh
bicycle (m)	*bicyclette, vélo*	bicycle
bicycle à gaz	*motocyclette*	motorcycle
aller en bicycle	*. . . à bicyclette*	to ride a bicycle
billet d'autobus (m)	*ticket*	ticket
bout de la ligne (m)	*terminus*	end of the line (train)
brochure (f)	*dépliant*	brochure
canot (m)	*canoë*	canoe
faire du canotage	*faire du canoë, du bateau*	to go canoeing, to go boating
carriole, catherine (f)	*traîneau*	sleigh
carrosse (m)	*poussette, voiture d'enfant*	baby buggy, baby carriage
chaland (m)	*petite embarcation*	flat bottom boat
chaloupe (f)	*barque*	rowboat
char à bagages (m)	*fourgon*	baggage car
char à dîner	*wagon-restaurant*	dining car
char à fret	*wagon-marchandise*	freight car
char à malle	*wagon-poste*	mail car
char à passagers	*voiture à voyageurs*	passenger car
petits chars (pl)	*tramway*	street car

Canada	**France**	
gros chars (pl)	*train*	train
chauffeur d'autobus (m)	*conducteur d'autobus*	bus driver
cométique (m)	*traîneau à chiens*	dog sleigh
conducteur (m)	*chef de train, contrôleur*	conductor
débarquer (d'un char, d'un train)	*descendre*	to get out, off
dépôt d'autobus (m)	*terminus*	bus depot
embarquer (dans un char, dans un train)	*monter*	to get in, on
envolée (f)	*vol*	flight
gaz (m), gazoline (f)	*essence*	gas, gasoline
goélette (f)	*caboteur*	small fishing or logging boat
lift (m), occasion (f) (donner une occasion à qn)	*faire monter qn dans sa voiture*	lift (to give s.o. a lift)
vol nolisé (m)	*charter*	chartered flight
noliser un avion, un autobus	*louer*	to charter a plane, bus
océanique (m)	*transatlantique*	ocean liner
passager (dans les trains et autobus) (m)	*voyageur*	passenger
pompeur (m)	*draisine*	jigger, handcar
plate-forme, voie (f)	*quai*	platform, track
portage, portageage (m)	*portage d'un canoë d'un cours d'eau à un autre*	portage
portager	*faire un "portage"*	to portage
faire du pouce, poucer, voyager sur le pouce	*faire de l'auto-stop, voyager en auto-stop*	to hitch-hike, to thumb
pouceux (m)	*auto-stoppeur*	hitch-hiker
rame (f)	*aviron, pagaie*	oar, paddle
réacté (m)	*avion à réaction*	jet
réserver une place	*retenir une place*	to reserve a seat
route d'autobus (f)	*ligne d'autobus*	bus route
stand de taxis (m)	*station de taxis*	taxi stand
station de gaz (f)	*poste d'essence, station-service*	gas station, service station

Canada	France	
(terrain de) stationnement (m)	*parking*	parking lot
système de transit (m)	*système de transport*	transit system
train local (m), train de banlieue (m)	*train omnibus*	local train, suburban train
transfert (m)	*correspondance*	transfer
traque (f)	*rails, voie ferrée*	(railroad) track
traverse (de chemin de fer) (f)	*passage à niveau*	(level) crossing
traverse (f)	*endroit où on prend le bac*	crossing point (for ferry)
traversier (m)	*bac, ferry-boat*	ferry(boat)
truck (m)	*camion*	truck
vanne (f)	*camion-remorque*	(moving) van
voyagement (m)	*allées et venues*	running about, travelling
yacht (m)	*(bateau) hors-bord*	motorboat

L'Automobile (The Automobile)

Canada	France	
ajuster	*régler*	to adjust, to set
ajustage (m)	*réglage*	adjustment, setting
auto (m,f), char (m), machine (f)	*voiture, bagnole*	car
auto-lave, lave-auto (m)	*lavage d'autos*	car wash
balancement (des roues) (m)	*équilibrage*	(wheel) balancing
batterie (f)	*accumulateur, accus*	battery
bazou (m), minoune (f), paquet de ferraille (m), touffe (f)	*tacot, vieille voiture*	old heap, jalopy, wreck
billet, ticket (m)	*contravention*	ticket
brake, bréke (m)	*frein*	brake
bréke à bras (m)	*frein à main*	handbrake
bréker, mettre les brékes	*freiner*	to brake, put on the brakes
bumpeur (m)	*pare-chocs*	bumper
cap de roue (m)	*enjoliveur*	hubcap
changer l'huile	*vidanger l'huile*	to change the oil
chauffer	*conduire*	to drive
chaufferette (f)	*chauffage*	heater
chirer, skidder	*déraper, patiner*	to skid
choke, étrangleur (m)	*starter*	choke
citron (m)	*voiture en mauvais état*	lemon
clotche (f)	*embrayage*	clutch
convertible (m)	*décapotable*	convertible
cramper	*braquer les roues*	to turn the wheels
criard (m)	*klaxon*	horn
dash (m)	*tableau de bord*	dashboard

Canada	France	
débarquer	*descendre*	to get out
démonstrateur (m)	*voiture d'essai*	demonstrator
école de conduite (f)	*auto-école*	driving school
embarquer	*monter*	to get in
s'embourber	*se prendre dans la neige*	to get stuck in the snow
flasheur (m)	*clignotant*	(turn) signal, signal light
flat (m)	*crevaison, pneu à plat*	flat (tire)
forces (f,pl)	*chevaux-vapeur*	horsepower
gaz (m), gazoline (f)	*essence*	gas, gasoline
donner du gaz, peser sur le gaz	*accélérer*	to step on the gas
gazer	*prendre de l'essence*	to get gas
générateur (m)	*dynamo*	generator
hiveriser, hiverniser	*préparer pour l'hiver*	to winterize
ivressomètre (m)	*alcoolmètre*	breathalyzer
jack (m)	*cric*	jack
jaune, régulier (m)	*ordinaire*	regular (gas)
licence (f)	*permis de conduire; plaque d'immatriculation*	(driver's) licence; (licence) plate
lumière (f), réflecteur (m)	*phare*	headlight
millage (m)	*kilométrage*	mileage
morceau (m), partie (f)	*pièce*	(spare) part
muffleur (m)	*silencieux*	muffler
au neutre	*au point mort*	in neutral, out of gear
parcomètre (m)	*parkmètre*	parking meter
partir (un char)	*démarrer, faire partir*	to start (a car)
pneu à neige, pneu de neige	*pneu d'hiver, pneu neige*	snow tire
raculer, reculer	*faire marche arrière*	to back up
en raque	*en ruine; en panne*	wrecked; broken down

67

Canada	France	
reconditionner	*remettre à neuf*	to recondition
remplir	*faire le plein*	to fill her up
renverse (f)	*marche arrière*	reverse
réparages (m,pl)	*réparations*	repairs
roue (f), steering (m)	*volant*	steering wheel
roue en broche	*roue à rayons*	mag wheel
rouge (m)	*super*	super, high test (gas)
scraper (un char)	*envoyer à la ferraille*	to wreck, to scrap (a car)
scrépeur (m)	*grattoir*	scraper
spare, spére (m)	*roue de secours*	spare (tire)
sprigne (m)	*ressort*	spring
stâler	*caler*	to stall
starteur (m)	*démarreur*	starter
station wagon (m)	*familiale, break*	station wagon
stationner (un char)	*garer, parquer*	to park (a car)
stationner	*se garer*	to park
steering (m)	*direction*	steering
être stoqué	*rester pris*	to be stuck
tank (f)	*réservoir*	gas tank
tire (m)	*pneu*	tire
touer	*remorquer*	to tow
touage (m)	*remorquage*	towing
towing (m)	*dépanneuse*	tow truck
transmission (f)	*boîte de vitesses*	transmission
un Chevrolet, un Ford, etc.	*une Chevrolet, une Ford*	a Chev, a Ford, etc.
usagé, e	*d'occasion*	used (car)
valise (f)	*coffre*	trunk
virage en U (m)	*demi-tour*	U turn
virer	*tourner*	to turn
virer de bord	*revenir sur ses pas*	to turn around
windshield (m)	*pare-brise*	windshield
wipeur (m)	*essuie-glace*	windshield wiper

Gouvernement et Elections (Government and Elections)

Partis politiques (Political Parties)

Canada

bleus (m)	Tories
Crédit Social, Ralliement des Créditistes (m)	Social Credit
créditiste (m)	Creditiste
créditisme (m)	Social Credit doctrine
fédéral (m), gouvernement fédéral (m)	Ottawa, federal government
Nouveau Parti Démocratique (NPD); néo-démocrate, social-démocrate (m)	New Democratic Party (NDP); New Democrat, NDPer
oppositionniste (m)	member of the opposition
Parti (progressiste-) conservateur; (progressiste) conservateur, (progressiste) conservatrice	(Progressive) Conservative Party; Conservative
Parti libéral; libéral, e	Liberal Party; Liberal
Parti Québécois, PQ; péquiste	Parti Québécois; member or supporter of Parti Québécois
provincial, gouvernement provincial (m)	the province, provincial government
rouges (m)	Grits
Union nationale (f); unioniste	Union Nationale; member or supporter of the Union Nationale

Postes (Positions)

Canada	France	
auditer	*vérifier*	to audit
auditeur (m)	*vérificateur*	auditor
auditeur général	*commissaire aux comptes*	Auditor General
chef parlementaire, leader gouvernemental (m)	*porte-parole d'un parti*	parliamentary leader
chef de cabinet (m)	*conseiller spécial du premier ministre*	Secretary to the Cabinet
commissaire (m)	*membre du comité exécutif*	controller (board of control)
conseiller de la Reine (m)	*titre honorifique pour un avocat*	Queen's Counsel
contrôleur du Trésor (m)	*vérificateur du Trésor*	Comptroller of the Treasury
échevin (m)	*conseiller municipal*	alderman
échevinage (m)		aldermanship
employé civil, employé civique (m)	*fonctionnaire municipal*	civic employee
Gentilhomme huissier de la verge noire (m)		Gentleman Usher of the Black Rod
Gouverneur-général, vice-roi (m)		Governor General
greffier de la ville (m)	*secrétaire général de la mairie*	City Clerk
greffier de la chambre	*secrétaire général de la "Chambre"*	Clerk of the House
l'honorable	*Monsieur le Ministre*	the Honourable
son honneur le maire	*Monsieur le Maire*	His Worship the Mayor
légiste (aux Communes) (m)	*greffier*	law clerk in the House
lieutenant-gouverneur (m)		Lieutenant-Governor

Canada	France	
membre du Parlement (m)	*député*	M.P.
officier-rapporteur (m)	*président d'élection*	returning officer
sous-officier-rapporteur (m)	*scrutateur*	deputy returning officer
orateur, président (m)		Speaker (of the House)
orateur suppléant, vice-président (m)		Deputy Speaker
Pères de la Confédération (m)	*membres fondateurs de la confédération canadienne*	Fathers of Confederation
politicien (m)	*homme politique*	politician
préfet (m) préfecture (f) sous-préfet (m)	*"maire" d'un comté*	reeve reeveship deputy reeve
premier ministre (m)	*premier ministre du "Fédéral" ou des provinces*	Prime Minister, premier
premier secrétaire (m)	*conseiller spécial d'un ministre*	First Secretary
procureur général (m)	*ministre de la justice*	Attorney General
receveur général du Canada (m)	*trésorier du gouvernement*	Receiver General of Canada
secrétaire d'Etat (m)	*Ministre de l'Intérieur*	Secretary of State
secrétaire d'Etat adjoint		Assistant Under-Secretary of State
secrétaire parlementaire (m)	*aide parlementaire d'un ministre*	parliamentary secretary
sénateur (m)	*sénateur fédéral*	senator
solliciteur général (m)	*homme de loi qui assiste le procureur général*	Solicitor General
sous-ministre (m)	*ministre adjoint*	deputy minister
sous-ministre adjoint	*ministre adjoint auxiliaire*	assistant deputy minister
whip (m)	*sorte de chef de file*	whip

Divers (Miscellaneous)

Canada	France	
acte de l'Amérique du Nord britannique (m)	*constitution canadienne*	British North America Act
acte du parlement (m)	*loi adoptée au parlement*	Act of Parliament
administration (f)	*gouvernement au pouvoir*	the Administration (federal)
adresse (f)	*discours, remarques*	address, speech
agences (f)	*organismes*	agencies
agenda (m)	*ordre du jour*	agenda
jurer allégeance (f)	*. . . obéissance*	to swear allegiance
année fiscale, année financière (f)	*exercice financier*	fiscal year
appropriation (f.)	*crédits*	appropriation
Assemblée Nationale (f)	*assemblée nationale du Québec*	Quebec National Assembly
assurance-chômage (f)	*assurance contre le chômage*	unemployment insurance
assurance-santé (f)	*assurance-maladie*	health insurance
balance du pouvoir (f)	*charnière des partis*	balance of power
barre de la chambre (f)	*verge symbolique pour l'ouverture du parlement*	Bar of the House
bien-être social (m)	*assistance sociale*	welfare
être sur le bien-être	*être assisté social*	to be on welfare
bill (m)	*projet de loi*	bill
bill privé (m)	*projet de loi d'intérêt privé*	private bill
livre blanc, papier blanc (m)	*publication gouvernementale qui donne des renseignements sur une politique éventuelle*	white paper
bref (m)	*dossier, mémoire*	brief
bureau des commissaires, comité exécutif (m)		Board of Control

Gouvernement et Elections (Government and Elections)

Canada	France	
bureau de scrutin, bureau de votation, poll (m)	*bureau de vote*	poll
cabale (f)	*porte-à-porte, activité politique*	canvassing, political activity
cabaler	*faire du porte-à-porte, faire de la politique*	to canvass, to be involved in political action
cabaleur (m)	*démarcheur, ...*	canvasser, politically involved individual
canton (m), commune (f)	*division territoriale*	township
caucus (m)	*réunion à huis clos*	caucus
Centre de Main d'oeuvre (du Canada) (m)	*bureau de placement*	Canada Manpower Centre
certificat de naissance (m)	*acte de naissance*	birth certificate
chambre basse (f)	*assemblée législative*	Lower House
chambre haute	*sénat*	Upper House
Chambre des Communes, Communes	*chambre des députés*	House of Commons, Commons
chefferie (f)	*leadership*	leadership
(centre) civique	*municipal*	civic (centre)
(réception) civique	*officielle*	civic (reception)
colline (parlementaire) (f)	*emplacement en pente du gouvernement canadien*	(Parliament) Hill
comité de citoyens (m)	*comité qui étudie certains problemes des citoyens*	Citizens' Committee
Compagnie des Jeunes Canadiens (f)	*organisation fédérale qui appuie divers projets de la jeunesse*	Company of Young Canadians
comté (m)	*circonscription*	riding
(commission, rapport) de conciliation	*d'arbitrage*	Conciliation (Board, Report)
non-confiance (motion de, vote de)	*motion de censure*	motion, vote of non-confidence

Canada	France	
(comité) conjoint	*(comité) mixte*	joint (committee)
conseil de ville (m)	*conseil municipal*	City Council
convention de chefferie, de leadership (f)	*congrès d'investiture*	leadership convention
corporation (d'une ville) (f)	*gouvernement (municipal)*	corporation (of a city)
département (m)	*ministère*	department
dépendant, e	*personne à charge*	dependent
discours du budget (m)	*discours important donné à la présentation du budget*	budget speech
discours du trône (m)	*discours du président du conseil*	Throne speech
disparités régionales (f)	*inégalités entre les "provinces"*	regional disparities
distribution des pouvoirs (f)	*partage des pouvoirs*	distribution of powers
édifice de l'est (m)	*bâtiment du gouvernement fédéral*	East Block
élection (f)	*élections*	election (for a government)
élection complémentaire, partielle (f)	*élection de remplacement*	by-election
électorat (m)	*corps électoral*	electorate
d'état (dîner, funérailles)	*officiel; national*	state (dinner, funeral)
franchise (f)	*droit de vote*	franchise
travailler au gouvernement	*être fonctionnaire*	to work for the government
hansard (m)	*journal officiel des débats*	Hansard
homologuer	*empêcher la construction d'un édifice sur un terrain d'intérêt public*	to expropriate land, to rezone land
identification (f)	*pièces d'identité, papiers*	papers, identification

Canada	France	
indépendantisme (m); indépendantiste (m)	*doctrine politique pour l'indépendance du Québec; partisan de cette doctrine*	separatism; separatist
informateur, rice	*dénonciateur*	informer
initiatives locales (f)	*organisation fédérale qui subventionne des particuliers pour créer des emplois*	local initiatives
juridiction (fédérale, provinciale) (f)	*compétence*	jurisdiction (federal, provincial)
lecture (d'un bill) (f)	*prise en considération d'un "bill"*	reading (of a bill)
législation (f)	*loi*	legislation
législature (f)	*gouvernement*	legislature
métropolitain (gouvernement, conseil)	*d'une grande ville*	metropolitan (gov't, council)
municipalité régionale (f)		regional municipality
mise en nomination (f)	*désignation*	nomination
Nouveaux Horizons (m)	*programme d'aide aux vieillards*	New Horizons
office de la protection du consommateur (m)		Consumers' Protection Bureau
ordre en conseil (m)	*arrêté ministériel, décret*	order in Council
ouverture du Parlement (f)	*rentrée*	Opening of Parliament
parachutage (m) (d'un candidat)	*désignation dans une circonscription propice d'un candidat étranger au comté*	parachuting
Parlement, édifice parlementaire (m)	*Hôtel du Gouvernement*	Parliament, Parliament Buildings
paroisse (f)	*commune*	parish, township

Canada	France	
partisanerie (f)	*esprit de parti*	party politics, partisan politics
passer (une loi)	*voter*	to pass (a law)
patronage (m)	*favoritisme*	patronage
payeur de taxes (m)	*contribuable*	taxpayer
pension de vieillards, pension de vieillesse (f)	*retraites de vieillesse*	old age pension
péréquation (f)	*subventions fédérales pour égaliser les richesses des provinces*	equalization grants
période des réponses (f)		answer period (for throne speech, etc.)
Perspectives Jeunesse (f)	*organisme fédéral qui appuie divers projets de la jeunesse*	Opportunities for Youth Program
planification régionale (f)		regional planning
plan de pension (m)	*régime de retraite*	pension plan
politicaillerie (f)	*petite politique mesquine*	petty politics
politicailleur (m)	*celui qui fait de la petite politique mesquine*	small-time politician
politique de bouts de chemin (f)	*politique qui consiste à acheter des votes en faisant construire des routes dans une circonscription*	policy of obtaining votes by promising to build roads, etc.
province (f); provincial, e; droits provinciaux (m)	*division administrative du Canada . . .*	province; provincial; provincial rights
recomptage (m)	*addition de voix*	recount
régistraire général du Canada (m)	*secrétariat du gouvernement*	Registrar General of Canada
redistribution (f)	*remaniement (de la carte électorale)*	redistribution (of seats)

Gouvernement et Elections (Government and Elections)

Canada	France	
serment d'office (m)		oath of office
service civil (m)	*fonction publique*	civil service
être en session	*être en séance*	to be in session
Société de la Couronne (f)	*Société d'Etat*	Crown Corporation
sortant (conseiller etc.)	*actuel*	incumbent (councillor etc.)
statut civil (m)	*état civil*	civil status
statut social (m)	*rang social*	social status
suiveux, euse	*partisan aveugle*	yes man
taxation (f)	*impôts*	taxation
village policé (m)	*village ou ville sans "corporation"*	police village
voteur (m)	*votant*	voter
vote populaire (m)	*vote national*	popular vote
virer son capot	*changer de parti politique*	to change sides
vire-capot (m)		turncoat, maverick
zoner	*soumettre à un règlement de zonage*	to zone

Travail et Industrie (Work and Industry)

Métiers (Jobs)

Canada	France	
agent de réclamation, ajusteur (m)	*expert (en évaluation)*	adjuster
artiste commercial (m)	*dessinateur publicitaire*	commercial artist
assistant (gérant, etc.)	*adjoint; aide*	assistant (manager, etc.)
assureur (assureur-vie, etc.) (m)	*agent d'assurances*	(life, etc.) insurance agent
auditeur (m)	*vérificateur-comptable*	auditor
barbier (m)	*coiffeur*	barber
bartender (m)	*barman*	bartender
bonceur (m)	*videur*	bouncer
bourreur, rembourreur (m)	*tapissier en ameublement*	upholsterer
brigade du feu, des incendies (f)	*corps des pompiers*	fire brigade
briqueleur (m)	*briqueteur*	bricklayer
briqueler	*briqueter*	to lay bricks
bûcheur, bûcheux, homme de chantier (m)	*bûcheron*	lumberjack; woodcutter
chansonnier (m)	*interprète-compositeur*	song writer and singer
entrer en charge	*assumer son travail*	to take up one's duties
être en charge de, responsable de	*être préposé à*	to be in charge of
chef des pompiers (m)	*pompier en chef*	fire chief
chiropraticien (m)	*chiropracteur*	chiropractor
col (collet) blanc (m)	*employé de bureau*	white-collar worker
col bleu	*ouvrier spécialisé*	blue-collar worker

Canada	France	
collecteur (m)	*agent de recouvrement; percepteur; contrôleur*	debt, bill collector; tax-collector; ticket collector
colon (m)	*défricheur*	farmer, homesteader
commis de bar (m)	*serveur, vendeur*	bar clerk
commis de bureau	*commis*	office clerk
commis d'épicerie, de pharmacie, etc.	*petit employé*	grocery, drug store clerk
comptable agréé (m)	*expert comptable*	chartered accountant
conducteur (m)	*receveur, chef de train*	conductor (on train)
conseiller en orientation (m)	*orienteur*	guidance counsellor
travailler dans (sur) la construction	*travailler dans le bâtiment*	to be a construction worker
contracteur, jobbeur (m)	*entrepreneur à forfait*	contractor
sous-contracteur	*sous-entrepreneur*	sub-contractor
contracteur général	*entrepreneur à tout faire*	general contractor
cotiseur, évaluateur (m)	*estimateur*	evaluator
coureur de bois (m)	*trappeur de la Nouvelle-France*	coureur de bois
courtier (m)	*agent de change*	(stock) broker
courtier d'immeubles, courtier en valeurs immobilières	*agent d'immeubles, marchand de biens*	real estate agent
cultivateur, habitant (m)	*fermier, agriculteur*	farmer
curateur (m)	*conservateur*	curator
débardeur (m)	*docker*	longshoreman
débosser	*travailler comme tôlier*	to do bodywork
débossage (m)	*tôlerie*	bodywork
débosseur (m)	*tôlier*	body-shop worker, bodyman
directeur général (m)	*directeur supérieur*	director general

Canada	France	
dispatcheur (m)	*"dispatcher" pour les camions*	dispatcher
draveur, cageux, raftman (m)	*flotteur*	raftsman, logger
embouteilleur (m)	*compagnie qui met en bouteilles les eaux gazeuses*	(soft drink) bottling company
employé (m)	*salarié*	employee (of company)
encan (m)	*vente aux enchères*	auction (sale)
encanter	*vendre aux enchères*	to auction off
encanteur (m)	*commissaire-priseur*	auctioneer
exécutif (m)	*chef d'entreprise*	executive
fâreman, foreman (m)	*contremaître*	foreman
fille, garçon de bureau	*coursière, coursier*	office girl, boy
fille engagée, engagère	*bonne*	maid, housegirl
fourrurier (m)	*fourreur*	furrier
garçon d'ascenseur (m)	*liftier*	elevator attendant
garde (f)	*garde-malade*	nurse
garde-feu (m)	*garde forestier*	forest ranger, fire warden
gérant (m)	*directeur; imprésario; manager*	manager (in all types of businesses)
gérant général	*directeur en chef*	general manager
gérant de banque	*directeur . . .*	bank manager
gérant de production	*responsable de la fabrication*	production manager
gérant des ventes	*directeur commercial*	sales manager
guenillou (m)	*marchand de chiffons; mendiant*	rag man; beggar
helpeur (m)	*aide*	helper
hobo (m)	*vagabond*	hobo
homme engagé (m)	*valet de ferme*	hired man
incorporé, e (compagnie)	*constitué*	incorporated

Canada	France	
incorporation (d'une compagnie)	*constitution*	incorporation (of a company)
infirmière licenciée (f)	*infirmière attitrée*	registered nurse
aide-infirmière, auxiliaire (f)	*infirmière qui assiste l'infirmière attitrée*	nurses' aide
ingénieur (m)	*mécanicien*	engineer (train)
ingénieur professionnel	*ingénieur*	professional engineer
job, jobbe, djobbe (f)	*job (m)*	job
jobbine (f)	*petit travail*	small job, odd job
jobbeur (m)	*intermédiaire; entrepreneur; travailleur à la pièce*	middleman, retailer; contractor; piece worker
journalier (m)	*manoeuvre, homme de peine*	labourer
junior	*secondaire, petit*	junior (clerk, etc.)
senior	*premier, principal*	senior
laveur de vaisselle (m)	*plongeur*	dishwasher
licencié (électricien, etc.)	*breveté, patenté*	licensed (electrician, etc.)
limitée (ltée)	*Cie, société anonyme*	. . . limited
magicien (m)	*prestidigitateur*	magician
maître de poste (m)	*receveur*	postmaster
marchand (m)	*commerçant*	merchant
marchand de fer	*quincaillier*	hardwareman
marchand de glace; marchand de crème à glace	*glacier*	iceman; ice cream man
marchand de gros	*grossiste*	wholesaler
marchand de seconde main	*brocanteur*	second-hand dealer
marchand de tabac, tabaconiste (m)	*buraliste*	tobacconist
mécanique (m)	*mécanicien*	mechanic
ménagère (f)	*maîtresse de maison; femme de charge*	housewife; housekeeper
meublier (m)	*marchand de meubles; ébéniste*	furniture dealer, maker

81

Canada	France	
modiste (f)	*couturière*	dressmaker
moulignier (m)	*meunier*	miller
nettoyeur (à sec) (m)	*teinturier*	dry cleaner
nursing (m)	*sciences infirmières*	nursing
officier (m)	*représentant, fonctionnaire; douanier*	official (administrative); (customs) officer
opérateur (m), opératrice (f)	*technicien, ouvrier*	machine operator
optométriste (m)	*spécialiste de la vue*	optometrist
orfèvre (m)	*horloger-bijoutier*	jeweller
outilleur (m)	*technicien qui confectionne les matrices de machines-outils*	tool and die maker
ouvrier (m)	*menuisier*	carpenter
ouvrier général	*ouvrier à tout faire*	general help
paie-maître (m)	*payeur*	paymaster
paysagiste (m)	*architecte paysagiste*	landscaper
peddleur (m)	*colporteur*	peddler
physiothérapeute, physiothérapiste (m)	*celui qui soigne les maladies à l'aide d'aliments naturels*	physiotherapist
pilote de brousse (m)	*pilote dans le Nord canadien*	bush pilot
placier (m), placière (f)	*ouvreuse*	usher, usherette
plâtreur (m)	*plâtrier*	plasterer
poinçonner, puncher	*pointer*	to punch (in and out)
porteur de journaux (m)	*vendeur, petit camelot*	paperboy
postier, postillon (m)	*facteur*	mailman, postman
presseur, presseuse (f)	*repasseur*	presser
privé, e (secrétaire, etc.)	*particulier*	private (secretary)

Canada	France	
professionnel, elle	*spécialisé*	professional (lawyer, doctor, etc.)
professionnel (m)	*membre des professions libérales*	professional (person)
ramancheur (m)	*rebouteur*	bone setter
réceptionniste (f)	*préposée à la réception*	receptionist
régulier (emploi)	*habituel*	regular (job)
réhabilitateur (m)	*conseiller*	rehabilitator
salaire (m)	*traitement, appointements*	salary
scientiste (m)	*homme de science, savant*	scientist
scrapeur, vendeur de scrap (m)	*casseur*	scrap yard owner, auto wrecker
servante (f)	*domestique*	maid, servant
shippeur (m)	*expéditeur*	shipper
solliciteur (m)	*démarcheur, placier*	solicitor
sucrier (m)	*fabricant de sucre d'érable*	maple sugar maker
superviseur (m)	*surveillant*	supervisor
surintendant (m)	*directeur, surveillant*	superintendent
tapissage (m)	*tapisserie*	paper hanging
tapisseur (m)	*tapissier*	paper hanger
tôleur, travailleur du métal en feuille (m)	*tôlier*	sheet-metal worker
travaillant (m)	*travailleur*	worker; hard worker
travailleur social (m)	*assistant social*	social worker
tuileur (m)	*carreleur*	tile layer
tuyauteur (m)	*installateur de tuyaux*	pipe fitter
vidangeur (m)	*boueur*	garbageman
waiter (m), waitress (f)	*garçon, serveuse*	waiter, waitress

Divers (Miscellaneous)

Canada	France	
accrédité, e	*agréé*	accredited
acter	*jouer*	to act (in a play)
amalgamer	*fusionner*	to amalgamate (companies)
s'ambitionner	*travailler dur*	to work hard
applicant (m)	*postulant, candidat*	applicant
application (f)	*demande d'emploi*	application
faire (une) application, appliquer	*faire une demande d'emploi*	to apply
associé (adj. et nom)	*compagnon de travail; adjoint; partenaire*	associate
autorisé, e	*attitré*	authorized
bardasseux (m)	*homme à tout faire*	jack of all trades
bénéfices (m)	*indemnités, prestations*	benefits
boss (m)	*patron, chef*	boss
botcher	*bousiller*	to bungle a piece of work
botchage (m)	*bousillage*	poorly done work
botcheur (m)	*bousilleur*	bungler
break (m), récréation (f)	*pause*	break (coffee, etc.)
bureau chef (m)	*bureau principal, siège social*	head office
bureau des directeurs (m)	*conseil d'administration*	Board of Directors
business (f)	*métier; entreprise*	business (job; enterprise)
être business	*être bon en affaires*	to be a good businessman
carré (en affaires)	*honnête et habile*	honest (in business)
carte de temps (f)	*feuille de présence*	timecard
caserne de pompiers, station de feu (f)	*poste d'incendie*	fire hall

Canada	France	
chambre de commerce (f)	*chambre économique*	Board of Trade, Chamber of Commerce
chantier (m)	*exploitation forestière*	lumber camp
chef-d'oeuvreux, euse	*habile*	handy, skilled
chiffe, chiffre, shift, quart (m)	*poste, équipe*	shift
comité conjoint (m)	*commission paritaire*	joint committee
comité exécutif	*comité directeur*	executive committee
marque de commerce (f)	*... de fabrique*	brand name
rue commerciale (f)	*rue commerçante*	commercial street, business street
compagnie de finance (f)	*société de crédit*	finance company
Confédération des Syndicats Nationaux (CSN) (f)		Confederation of National Trade Unions (CNTU)
Congrès du Travail du Canada (CTC) (m)		Canadian Labour Congress (CLC)
co-op (f)	*coopérative*	co-operative, co-op
corporation (f)	*compagnie, société*	corporation
corvée (f)	*prestation gratuite*	bee (barn raising, wood bee, etc.)
cour de bois (f)	*dépôt de bois, scierie*	lumberyard
crédit aux consommateurs (m)	*crédit de consommation*	consumers' credit
démotion (f)	*rétrogradation*	demotion
département du personnel (m)	*bureau d'embauchage*	personnel department
dépenses capitales (f)	*dépenses en immobilisation*	capital expenditures
en devoir	*de service*	on duty
dompeuse (f)	*benne*	dump truck
drave (f)	*flottage*	log drive
éligible à	*admissible à*	eligible for
faire une embardée	*faire une mauvaise affaire*	to make a mistake (in business)
être à l'emploi de ...	*travailler pour ...*	to work for (a company)

Canada	France	
entraîné, e	*formé*	trained
entraînement (m)	*formation*	training
réentraînement (m)	*recyclage*	(job) retraining
estimé (m)	*estimation, devis*	estimate
extra (m)	*supplément de travail; supplément de marchandise*	extra (time); extras
travailler d'extra, faire de l'overtime, du surtemps	*faire des heures supplémentaires*	to work overtime
factrie (f)	*manufacture, fabrique*	factory
Fédération des Travailleurs du Québec (FTQ) (f)		Quebec Federation of Labour (QFL)
feuille de temps (f)	*feuille de présence*	time sheet
force ouvrière (f)	*main d'oeuvre, population active*	labour force
gages (f,pl); gagne (f)	*salaire*	wages, pay; earnings
gagne (f)	*profit*	profit
vieux gagne (m)	*économies*	savings
aller en grève	*faire la grève*	to go on strike
horloge-poinçon (f)	*horloge pointeuse*	time clock
travailler à la job, au morceau	*travailler à forfait, à la pièce*	to work on contract, to do piecework
jobber	*entreprendre à forfait; bousiller*	to work on contract; to bungle a piece of work
jour de semaine (m)	*jour ouvrable*	weekday, workday
ligne d'assemblage (f)	*chaîne de montage*	assembly line
local (m)	*section d'un syndicat*	local (of union)
malaxeur, mixeur (m)	*bétonnière*	cement mixer
maraudage (m)	*recrutement des membres chez un syndicat ouvrier rival*	(union) raiding
marque enregistrée (f)	*marque déposée*	registered trademark

Canada	France	
moulin à papier (m), pulperie (f)	*usine de papier*	(pulp and) paper mill
moulin à scie	*scierie*	sawmill
office (f)	*bureau*	office
ouverture (f)	*débouché*	(job) opening
de la belle ouvrage	*du travail bien fait*	a job well done
parc industriel (m)	*zone industrielle*	industrial park, zone
faire patate	*faire faillite*	to go bankrupt
partir un commerce	*lancer, fonder un commerce*	to start up a business
ligne de piquetage (f)	*piquet de grève*	picket line
piqueter; piqueteur (m)		to picket; picketer
plant (m)	*usine; succursale*	plant; branch
position (f)	*poste, situation*	position
pouvoir (m)	*centrale électrique*	powerplant
pratique (f)	*clientèle*	practice (of a lawyer)
projet (de construction) (m)	*ouvrage, chantier*	(construction) project
qualifications (f)	*diplôme; compétence*	qualifications
raboudiner	*bousiller*	to botch up
raboudinage (m)	*bousillage*	botched-up job
raboudineur (m)	*bousilleur*	botcher
route (de lait, etc.) (f)	*itinéraire*	route (milk, etc.)
royautés (f)	*redevances, droits d'auteur*	royalties
scab (m)	*jaune, briseur de grève*	scab, strikebreaker
shop (f)	*atelier; usine*	(machine) shop; plant
slaque (m)	*ralentissage*	slow time (in business)
slaquer	*mettre à pied*	to lay off
subsidiaire (f)	*filiale*	subsidiary
temps et demi (m)	*prime pour les heures supplémentaires*	time and a half

Canada	**France**	
transiger	*faire des affaires, des transactions*	to transact business
tue-monde (m)	*travail étouffant*	hard work
union (ouvrière) (f)	*syndicat (ouvrier)*	(trade) union
vaillant, e	*ardent au travail*	hard working

Le Bureau (The Office)

Canada	France	
affile-crayon, aiguisoir à crayon (m)	*taille-crayon*	pencil sharpener
affiler, aiguiser	*tailler*	to sharpen
agrafe, attache (f), clip (m), pince (f)	*trombone*	paper clip
babil, babillard (m)	*tableau d'affichage*	bulletin board
barbeau, barbot (m)	*tache d'encre*	(ink) blot
brocheuse (f)	*agrafeuse*	stapler
brocher	*agrafer*	to staple
cahier à anneaux (m)	*auto-relieur, classeur*	binder
compléter	*remplir*	to complete, fill out
crayon automatique (m)	*porte-mine*	eversharp, mechanical pencil, pen pencil
dactylo, dactylographe (m)	*machine à écrire*	typewriter
dernier nom (m)	*nom de famille*	last name
efface (f)	*gomme (à effacer)*	rubber, eraser
enregistreuse (f)	*magnétophone*	tape recorder
erreur cléricale (f)	*erreur matérielle*	clerical error
étampe (f)	*buvard; tampon*	blotter; rubber stamp
étamper	*timbrer*	to stamp
faire du bureau	*travailler dans un bureau*	to do office work
filière (f)	*classeur, fichier*	filing cabinet, file
fion (m)	*signature ornementée*	fancy signature
foolscap (m)	*papier ministre*	foolscap
forger une signature	*contrefaire ...*	to forge a signature

Canada	France	
formule (f)	*formulaire*	form
indentation (f)	*alinéa*	indented line
indexer	*mettre dans l'index*	to index
initialer	*parapher*	to initial
initiales (f)	*paraphe*	initials
mémo, mémorandum (m)	*note, message*	memo, memorandum
miméographe (f)	*duplicateur*	mimeograph
miméographier	*reproduire*	to mimeograph
minutes (f)	*procès-verbal*	minutes
papier indien (m)	*papier de Chine*	India paper
papier ligné	*papier réglé*	lined paper
papier oignon	*papier pelure*	onionskin
premier nom (m)	*prénom*	first name
plume-fontaine, -réservoir (f)	*stylo à encre*	fountain pen
plomb (m)	*mine*	lead (in pencil)
saucer une plume	*tremper une plume*	to dip a pen

Courrier et Lettres (Mail and Letters)

Adresses (Addresses)

Canada	France	
boîte postale (B.P.), case postale (f), casier postal (m) (C.P.)		Post Office Box (P.O. Box), Box
code postal		postal code
route rurale (f), (R.R.)		rural route (R.R.)
station, succursale (A,B, etc.) (f)		Station (A,B, etc.)

Divers (Miscellaneous)

à:, de:	destinataire:, expéditeur:	to:, from:
bien à vous, bien vôtre, sincèrement vôtre	je vous prie de croire à l'expression de mes sentiments distingués, etc.	yours sincerely, yours truly
boîte à malle (f)	boîte aux lettres	mailbox
charge postale (f)	frais de port	postage
Cher Monsieur	Monsieur	Dear Sir
classe (première, deuxième, troisième) (f)	tarif lettres, imprimés ...	(first, second, third) class
C.O.D.	C.R. (livraison contre remboursement)	C.O.D.
collection du courrier, de la malle (f)	levée ...	mail collection
enregistrer	recommander	to register

Courrier et Lettres (Mail and Letters)

Canada	France	
étampe (f)	*oblitération*	postmark
étamper	*oblitérer*	to stamp, to cancel
envoyer par exprès	*. . . messageries*	to send express (on train)
lettre morte (f)	*lettre de rebut*	dead letter
livraison générale (f)	*poste restante*	general delivery
livraison postale	*distribution du courrier*	postal delivery
livraison spéciale	*exprès*	special delivery
malle (f)	*courrier*	mail
maller	*mettre à la poste*	to mail
paquet (m)	*colis*	parcel
postier, postillon (m)	*facteur*	mailman, postman
sceller	*cacheter*	to seal (a letter, etc.)
timbre de huit sous, etc. (m)	*timbre à quarante centimes*	eight-cent stamp, etc.
zone postale (f)	*arrondissement, région*	postal zone

Moyens de Communication (Presse, Radio, Télévision)
Mass Media (Press, Radio, Television)

Canada	France	
agence de nouvelles (f)	*agence de presse*	news agency
album, long jeu (m)	*microsillon*	(record) album, LP
annoncer	*faire de la publicité*	to advertise
annonces classées (f)	*petites annonces*	classified ads, want ads
annonceur (m)	*speaker*	announcer
bonhommes, comiques (m,pl)	*bandes dessinées*	comics, comic strips
câble (m), câblodiffusion (f)	*télévision par câble coaxial*	cable TV, Cablevision
canal (m)	*chaîne, poste*	channel
chanson-thème (f)	*indicatif*	theme song
commanditer	*présenter, financer*	to sponsor
commanditaire (m)	*annonceur*	sponsor
commercial (m)	*annonce*	commercial
conférence de nouvelles (f)	*conférence de presse*	news conference
copie (f)	*exemplaire*	copy
écouter la télévision	*regarder . . .*	to watch TV
éditeur (m)	*rédacteur*	editor
endisquer	*enregistrer*	to record (a record)
gazette (f), papier (m)	*journal*	newspaper
émission à lignes ouvertes (f)	*émission où les auditeurs participent en -téléphonant*	call-in show, hot line show, open line show

Canada	France	
livraison (f)	*numéro*	issue
nouvelles (f,pl)	*informations*	(radio) news
palmarès (m)	*hit-parade*	hit parade
Radio·Canada		CBC
Radio-Mutuel; Télémédia		private radio networks
réseau (m)	*chaîne*	network, broadcasting company
statique (f)	*parasites*	static
syntoniser	*accrocher*	to tune in, to stay tuned to (a station)
Télé-Métropole		a private TV station
téléthéâtre (m)	*pièce télévisée, feuilleton*	TV play, serial
TV, tévé (f)	*télé*	TV
TVA		a private TV network

Le Téléphone (The Telephone)

Canada	France	
acoustique (m)	*récepteur*	receiver
appel à frais renversés, appel à frais virés (m)	*appel en P.C.V., communication payable à l'arrivée*	collect call
appel de personne à personne (m)	*appel en P.A.V., communication avec préavis*	person-to-person call
Qui appelle? Qui est sur la ligne? Qui parle?	*Qui est à l'appareil?*	Who's calling? Who's speaking?
assistance annuaire, information (f)	*renseignements*	directory assistance, information
code régional (m)	*indicatif*	area code
connecter	*mettre en communication*	to connect
connection (f)	*communication*	connection
engagé	*occupé*	busy
intercom, électrovox, télévox (m)	*interphone*	intercom
Gardez la ligne! Tenez la ligne!	*Ne quittez pas!*	Hold the line!
local (m)	*poste*	extension, local
longue distance (m)	*appel interurbain*	long distance call
opératrice (f)	*téléphoniste, standardiste*	operator
taper une ligne	*faire une prise sur une ligne*	to wiretap
téléphone (m)	*coup de fil coup de téléphone*	phone call
faire un téléphone, lâcher un téléphone	*passer un coup de fil*	to give a ring, make a call
ton du cadran (m)	*tonalité*	dial tone

L'Ecole (School)

Canada	France	
Académie (f)	*école*	Academy, school
(année) académique	*scolaire*	academic (year)
accélérer	*couvrir le programme d'études en moins de temps que la moyenne*	to accelerate
accélération (f)		acceleration
les Anciens (m)	*Anciens de l'Université*	Alumni
année (f), grade (m)	*classe; cycle*	year (of study), grade
annuaire (m), calendrier (m)	*bulletin, livret*	calendar (university)
assistance (f)	*présence*	attendance
atelier (m)	*assemblée pédagogique*	workshop
autobus d'écoliers, autobus scolaire (m)	*autobus, autocar, pour le transport des élèves; ramassage*	school bus
B.A. (m) (baccalauréat)	*licence*	B.A.
B.A. de spécialisation, spécialisé	*licence de quatre ans*	Honours B.A.
B.A. de trois ans	*licence de trois ans*	General, Pass B.A.
bal (m)	*bal dansant de fin d'année*	prom, formal, ball
bloquer, couler (un examen)	*échouer*	to flunk (an exam)
brevet (A,B) (m)	*diplôme attestant que son titulaire a le droit d'enseigner*	(Type A,B) certificate for teaching
carabin (m)	*étudiant*	university student

Canada	**France**	
cédule (f), horaire (m)	*emploi du temps*	timetable
CEGEP (Collège d'enseignement général et professionnel) (m); cégépien, ienne	*école polyvalente qui dispense un enseignement pré-universitaire ou technique, en deux ou trois années*	junior college in Quebec that precedes university or technical schools; CEGEP student
Centre d'apprentissage (en construction, etc.) (m)	*école d'enseignement pratique de certains métiers*	Training School, School of Apprenticeship
Centre d'études universitaires	*établissement dispensant une partie de l'enseignement supérieur*	University Extension
champ de concentration (m)	*matières principales*	field of concentration
chancelier (m)	*celui qui remet les diplômes à la "graduation" (titre honorifique)*	chancellor
chargé de cours (m)	*assistant*	lecturer
classe enrichie (f)	*classe avancée*	advanced, enriched class
classe-degré, classe du programme (f)		class, form, section (grade 10A, 10B, etc.)
cloche (f)	*sonnerie*	bell
collation de grades, graduation (f)	*fête des promotions*	graduation, commencement (ceremony)
collège (classique) (m)	*CEGEP sous l'ancien système*	former CEGEP and High School in Quebec, classical college
collège des Arts appliqués et de technologie	*école professionnelle*	College of Applied Arts and Technology
collégial (secondaire supérieur)	*du niveau du CEGEP*	The CEGEP level in Quebec

L'Ecole (School)

Canada	France	
commissaire (conseiller) régional (m)	*membre de la "Régionale"*	regional trustee (Quebec)
commissaire (conseiller) scolaire, d'école (m)		trustee; commissioner
commission (conseil) scolaire régionale, Régionale (f)	*corps public électif qui administre l'enseignement secondaire dans une "région" donnée*	elected board that administers high schools in each of the school regions of Quebec
commission (conseil) scolaire		school board, Board of Education
concours (m)	*examen*	exam
confrère (m)	*compagnon de classe*	classmate
conseil d'école (m), école des parents (f)	*association des parents d'élèves*	Parent Teacher Association (P.T.A.)
conseil des étudiants (m)		student council
conserver des points	*obtenir des points*	to get marks
conventum (m)	*réunion d'anciens élèves*	Alumni meeting
cours par correspondance, cours d'éducation permanente (m)		correspondence courses, extension courses, adult education courses
cours du soir		evening courses
cours de recyclage		retraining courses
cours de service		service courses
faire son cours secondaire, technique, scientifique, classique	*faire ses études secondaires, etc.*	to go to high school, etc.
C.P.E.S. (cours préparatoire aux études supérieures) (m)	*enseignement de transition (après la 11e année) qui permet d'accéder à l'université ou au CEGEP*	make-up year for the CEGEP or university

Canada	France	
crédit (m)	*cours qui compte pour l'obtention d'un diplôme*	credit
curriculum (m)	*programme d'études*	curriculum
cycle (m) (études de 2e, 3e cycle, etc.)	*série d'années au niveau primaire et secondaire*	division of grades in primary and secondary school (first "cycle" is first two years of high school)
demi-cours (m)	*cours d'un "demi-crédit"*	half course
département (m)	*institut*	department
interdépartemental, e		interdepartmental
dodger, foxer	*faire l'école buissonnière*	to play hooky, skip a class
dodge (f)		playing hooky, truancy
dodgeur (m)		truant
école primaire, publique, élémentaire (f)	*(école) primaire (1e degré)*	primary, public, elementary, school
école privée, confessionnelle, libre	*établissement dont l'administration ne relève pas d'un ministère*	private school
école publique	*école administrée par un organisme public*	public school
école secondaire (f), secondaire (m)	*lycée et collège*	high school
petite école, école de village (f)	*école avec une salle de classe*	one room school
école de métiers	*école professionnelle (C.E.T.)*	trade school
école moyenne d'agriculture	*école d'agronomie*	Agricultural College, School of Agriculture
école de réforme	*maison de redressement*	reform school
école séparée	*école libre*	separate school
écolier (m)	*élève*	primary school pupil

Canada	France	
éducation pour adultes (f)	*enseignement destiné aux adultes*	Adult Education
études graduées (f)	*études supérieures*	graduate studies
étudiant (m)	*élève*	student (at all levels)
étudiant universitaire	*étudiant*	university student
examen général (m)	*examen du doctorat*	comprehensive exam (Ph.D.)
examen de reprise	*examen de repêchage*	supplemental exam
Faculté des Arts (f)	*faculté des lettres*	Faculty of Arts
faillir	*échouer*	to fail
finissant (m)	*élève de dernière année*	student in his last year of study
génie (m) (civil, chimique, etc.)	*enseignement dans les grandes écoles ou les écoles spécialisées*	engineering (civil, chemical, etc.)
gradué (m)	*diplômé*	graduate
postgradué, e	*supérieur*	post-graduate
sous-gradué, e		undergraduate
école des gradués	*direction administrative des hautes études*	graduate school
humanités (f)	*sciences humaines*	humanities
immatriculation (f)	*bac*	senior matriculation
institut de technologie (cours technique) (m)	*lycée technique*	institute of technology
institut spécialisé (arts appliqués, etc.)	*grandes écoles*	specialized technical institute (applied arts, etc.)
institution (f)	*établissement*	institution
intramural, aux	*entre facultés*	intramural
jardin d'enfance (m)	*jardin d'enfants*	kindergarten
lettre de recommandation, lettre de référence (f)	*attestation*	letter of recommendation, of reference
leçon privée (f)	*leçon particulière*	private lesson

Canada	France	
professeur à la leçon (m)	*. . . payé "à la leçon"*	supply teacher
licence (f)	*à peu près l'équivalent de la maîtrise*	an approximate equivalent of the M.A.
local-classe, classe titulaire (f)	*salle de classe où les mêmes étudiants se retrouvent assez souvent*	home room
maison d'enseignement (f)	*établissement*	educational institution
maîtresse (f)	*institutrice*	female primary school teacher
maîtrise ès Arts, M.A. (f)	*maîtrise*	Master of Arts, M.A.
majeur, mineur (m)	*sujets de spécialisation*	major, minor
municipalité scolaire, régionale (f)	*territoire d'une "commission scolaire"*	school district
navot (m)	*bizuth*	freshman
option (f)	*matières choisies*	option; minor
passer	*réussir*	to pass
Ph.D. (m)	*Doctorat*	Ph.D.
philosophe (m)	*étudiant en dernière année de l'ancien "cours classique"*	student in last year of the former "cours classique"
Polytechnique (école polytechnique) (f)	*grandes écoles, école professionnelle*	Polytechnical Institute, school of engineering
Polyvalente (f)	*établissement qui offre de nombreuses options (professionnelles et générales); lycée*	composite school (equivalent of high school in Quebec)
post-secondaire, secondaire supérieur	*après le secondaire*	post-secondary
prendre un cours	*suivre un cours*	to take a course
prérequis (m)	*conditions préalables*	prerequisites
principal (m)	*directeur (école primaire), proviseur (lycée)*	principal

L'Ecole (School)

Canada	France	
professeur adjoint, professeur assistant (m)		assistant professor
professeur associé, professeur agrégé		associate professor
professeur titulaire		full professor; home room teacher (high school)
(année) propédeutique	*(année) préparatoire pour le "B.A."*	qualifying (year)
rester en punition	*être consigné*	to have a detention
régistraire (m)	*secrétaire*	registrar
relevé de notes (m)	*copie des notes au niveau universitaire*	transcript
répéter une classe	*redoubler une classe*	to repeat a class
résidence (des étudiants) (f)	*pavillon où résident les étudiants (cité universitaire)*	(students') residence
responsable d'étudiants (m)	*conseiller*	student counsellor, advisor
rhétoricien (m) (rhétorique) (f)	*étudiant en 6e année de l'ancien "cours classique", (ce programme)*	student in the 6th year of the former "cours classique" (6th year)
secondaire V (m)	*dernière année du lycée canadien*	fifth, last year of high school in Quebec
semestre (m)	*trimestre*	semester
sénat (m)	*conseil de l'université*	senate
spécialité, spécialisation (f), majeur (m), (combiné, e)	*concentration (en 2 matières)*	(combined) major
stagiaire (m)	*maître de salle d'étude*	T.A. (teaching assistant)
strappe, vardette (f)	*verge*	strap
taxe scolaire (m)	*taxe payée au "conseil scolaire"*	school tax
à temps partiel	*qui s'inscrit à une partie du programme*	part-time (student)

Canada	France	
à plein temps	*qui s'inscrit à tout le programme*	full-time
transport scolaire (m)	*ramassage*	bussing, transportation
tuteur (m)	*maître d'étude; conseiller*	tutor; guidance counsellor
vert (m)	*étudiant de première année*	first year student
vice-principal (m)		vice-principal
visiteur (m)	*inspecteur*	inspector

Forces Armées, Police (Armed Forces, Police)

Canada	France	
boeuf, chien, dick (m)	*flic, poulet*	cop, fuzz
brigadier (m)	*général de brigade*	brigadier
cadet (m)	*élève-officier*	cadet
conscription (f)	*service militaire*	conscription
constable (m)	*agent de police*	constable
chef constable	*directeur, commissaire*	police chief
force constabulaire (f)	*force policière*	constabulary
garde de sécurité (m)	*agent de sécurité*	security guard
gendarmerie royale (f)	*police fédérale*	R.C.M.P.
homme de police (m), une police	*agent de police*	policeman, cop
major (m)	*chef de bataillon*	major
major général	*général de division*	major general
manège militaire (m)	*salle d'exercices militaires*	drill hall
matrone (f)	*femme policière*	policewoman
officier (m)	*policier*	(police) officer
pépé (f)	*police du Québec*	Q.P.P., provies
police montée (f)	*police fédérale*	mounted police
police provinciale		provincial police
police de ville	*police municipale*	town police, city police
shérif (m)	*huissier*	sheriff
spotteur (m)	*agent qui donne les contraventions*	traffic policeman
Sûreté du Québec (f)	*police du Québec*	Quebec Provincial Police
vétéran (m)	*ancien combattant*	(war) veteran

Système Judiciaire (Judicial System)

Canada	France	
avocat de la Couronne, procureur de la Couronne (m)	*avocat de l'Etat*	Crown Prosecutor
assermentation (f)	*prestation de serment*	swearing in
assermenter	*faire prêter serment*	to swear in
aviseur légal, conseiller légal (m)	*conseiller juridique*	legal advisor
code criminel (m)	*code pénal*	criminal code
conseil de la reine (m)	*titre honorifique conféré à un avocat*	Queen's Counsel
droit commun, droit coutumier (m)		common law
être hors d'ordre	*enfreindre le règlement*	to be out of order
injonction de la cour (f)	*ordonnance*	court injunction
être sur le jury	*faire partie d'un jury*	to be on a jury
libelle (m)	*diffamation*	libel
libelleux, euse	*diffamatoire*	libellous
offense (f)	*infraction*	offence
offense mineure	*simple infraction*	minor offence
opinion légale (f)	*avis juridique*	legal opinion
ordre en conseil (m)	*décret-loi*	order in council
paraître, passer en cour	*comparaître en cour*	to go to court, appear in court
plaider coupable	*s'avouer coupable*	to plead guilty
preuve circonstancielle, de circonstance (f)	*preuve par présomption*	circumstantial evidence
rapports judiciaires (m)	*recueils de jurisprudence*	law reports

Canada	France	
sentence suspendue (f)	*condamnation avec sursis*	suspended sentence
solliciteur (m)	*conseiller juridique*	solicitor
témoin de la Défense (m)	*témoin à décharge*	Defence witness
témoin de la Couronne	*témoin à charge*	Crown witness
verdict (m)	*sentence*	verdict

Cours (Courts) *(approximate French equivalents are given)*

cour criminelle	*cour d'assises*	Criminal Court
cour juvénile	*tribunal pour enfants et adolescents*	Juvenile Court
cour martiale	*conseil de guerre*	Military Court
cour municipale	*tribunal de police*	Municipal Court
cour supérieure	*tribunal de Grande Instance*	Superior Court (Quebec)
cour suprême	*cour de cassation*	Supreme Court
cour du banc de la reine	*cour d'appel, tribunal de Jugement*	Court of the Queen's Bench
cour de l'Echiquier	*cour des Comptes*	Court of the Exchequer
cour de magistrat, cour provinciale	*tribunal d'Instance*	Magistrate's Court
cours des sessions de la paix	*tribunal de Grande Instance*	Court of general sessions of the peace

Animaux (Animals)

Canada	France	
bébite (f)	*insecte*	insect, bug
belette (f)	*hermine*	weasel
bête à patates, bétite à patates (f)	*doryphore*	potato bug
bête puante (f), putois (m)	*moufette, skunks*	skunk
bourbeau, criquet (m)	*grillon*	cricket
broquant (m)	*cerf*	stag
brûlot (m)	*mouche fine à morsure brûlante*	small mosquito; blackfly
buffle (m)	*bison*	buffalo
carcajou (m)	*blaireau*	badger
caribou (m)	*renne du Canada*	caribou
chat sauvage (m)	*raton laveur*	raccoon
chevreuil, chevreux (m)	*cerf de Virginie*	deer
chien esquimau (m)		husky
chien des prairies		prairie dog
citelle, gaufre (f), siffleux (m)	*marmotte du Canada*	groundhog, gopher
coquerelle (f)	*blatte*	cockroach
crigne (f)	*crinière*	horse's mane
culteux, patineur (m)	*hydromètre*	water spider
écureux (m)	*écureuil*	squirrel
frémille (f)	*fourmi*	ant
frémillière (f)	*fourmillière*	ant hill
glouton (m)	*carcajou*	wolverine
loup-marin (m)	*otarie*	(Harper) seal
maringouin (m)	*moustique*	mosquito
marsouin (m)	*béluga*	white whale
mouche à feu (m)	*luciole*	firefly
orignal (m)	*élan d'Amérique*	moose

Canada	France	
ouaouaron (m)	*grenouille mugissante*	bullfrog
panthère (f)	*puma*	mountain lion
passes (f)	*pistes*	(animal) tracks
pichou (m)	*loup-cervier*	lynx, wildcat
picouille (f)	*rosse*	old nag
porc-épic (m)	*hérisson*	hedgehog, porcupine
queue-de-poêlon (f)	*têtard*	tadpole, polliwog
renardière (f)	*ferme où on élève les renards*	fox farm
souris-chaude (f)	*chauve-souris*	bat
suisse (barré) (m)	*petit écureuil*	chipmunk

Oiseaux (Birds)

Canada	France	
alouette de mer (f)	*limicole*	shore bird
barnache (f)	*bernache cravant*	barnacle goose
bobolink, goglu (m)	*sorte de passereau*	bobolink
bois-pourri (m)	*engoulevent*	whip-poor-will
canard malard, canard français (m)	*canard colvaire*	mallard (duck)
cacaoui (m)	*harelde de Miquelon*	(oldsquaw) duck
étourneau (à tête brune) (m)	*vacher*	cowbird
fou de Bassan, margot (m)	*fou de Gaspé*	gannet (from the Gaspé)
Frédéric (cache-ton-cul) (m)	*sorte de frengillidé*	(white throated) sparrow
huard, huart (m)	*plongeon*	loon
kildi, kildir (m)	*pluvier*	kildeer
geai bleu (m)	*geai d'Amérique*	bluejay
grive (f), merle, rouge-gorge (m)	*grive d'Amérique*	robin
merle bleu (m)	*grive d'Amérique*	bluebird
moineau (m)	*moineau, petit oiseau*	sparrow, small bird
oriole (m)	*sorte de passereau*	(Baltimore) oriole
outarde (f)	*Bernache du Canada*	Canada goose
perdrix (f)	*Tétras des savanes, Gélinotte huppée*	spruce grouse, ruffed grouse
perdrix de bois franc, perdrix grise	*Tétras des savanes*	spruce grouse
pic-bois (m)	*pic*	woodpecker
piroche (f)	*cane*	duck
piron (m)	*caneton*	young duck
poule des Praires (f)	*tétraonidé d'Amérique*	prairie chicken
récollet (m)	*jaseur des cèdres*	(cedar) waxwing
voilier, volier (m)	*vol*	flock

Poissons (Fish)

Canada	France	
achigan (à grande bouche, à petite bouche, de roche) (m)	*perche commune*	bass (large mouth, small mouth, rock)
agrès de pêche (m,pl)	*nécessaire de pêche*	fishing tackle
aiguillot (m)	*roussette*	dogfish
aim, ain, croc (m)	*hameçon*	fish-hook
barbotte (f)	*poisson-chat*	catfish
castor (m)	*carpe*	carp
crapet (calico; gris) (m)	*perche*	(calico; rock) bass, crappie
crapet soleil	*poisson-lune*	sunfish
doré (jaune; noir) (m)	*brochet*	(yellow; black, walleyed) pike
garrot (m)	*poisson du Manitoba*	goldeye
goberge (f), haddeck, haddock, poisson de St-Pierre (m)	*aiglefin*	haddock
louche (f), (petit) poisson des chenaux, des Trois-Rivières (m), petite morue (f), poulamon (m)	*sorte de morue*	tomcod, frostfish
maskinongé (m)	*brochet*	muskellunge, musky
méné (m)	*vairon*	minnow
moulac (m)	*truite mouchetée*	splake
ouananiche (f)	*saumon d'eau douce*	(land locked) salmon, wananish
pêcher à la trôle	*pêcher à la cuiller*	to troll
perchaude (f)	*perche*	(yellow, soft water) perch
poisson blanc (m)	*sorte de merlan*	whitefish
saumon sockeye (m)	*saumon américain*	sockeye salmon
tenture (f)	*bordigue; seine*	dam to catch fish; draw net
vigneau (m)	*table pour faire sécher la morue; filet*	screen table to dry cod; net

Arbres et Plantes (Trees and Plants)

Canada	France	
babina, pimbina (m)	*fruit de la viorne*	fruit of the viburnum
bleuet (m)	*airelle*	blueberry
bûcher	*abattre*	to cut down (a tree)
buis (m), pruche (f)	*tsuga du Canada*	hemlock
catherinette (f)	*mûre*	blackberry
cèdre (m)	*thuya*	cedar
cédrière (f)	*forêt de thuyas*	cedar bush
cenellier, snellier (m)	*aubépine*	hawthorn
clajeux (petit cochon) (m)	*iris des champs (son fruit)*	yellow iris (its fruit)
cocotte (f)	*cône*	(pine, etc.) cone
cormier, mascau, mascou (m)	*fruit du sorbier*	fruit of the mountain ash
couenne (f)	*gazon*	grass
couenner (un parterre)	*poser le gazon*	to sod
coeurs saignants (m)	*coeurs de Marie*	bleeding hearts
cyprès (m)	*pin gris*	jackpine
épinette (f)	*épicéa*	spruce
érablière, sucrerie (f)	*peuplement d'érables*	maple bush, sugar bush
feuillu, e	*caduc*	deciduous
gauthérie couchée (f)	*thé des bois*	wintergreen
gomme de sapin (f)	*baume*	balsam (gum)
herbe à puce (f)	*sumac vénéneux*	poison ivy
navette (f)	*navet sauvage*	wild turnip
pénacs (m), patate en chapelet (f)	*apios d'Amérique*	ground nut
pétard (m)	*fleur de silène*	catch-fly
pétoune (f)	*aster*	aster
platane (f)	*sycamore*	sycamore

Arbres et Plantes (Trees and Plants)

Canada	France	
plaquebière (f)	*ronce-murier*	blackberry bush
pommetier (m)	*pommier de Sibérie*	crab apple tree
pommette (f)	*pomme de Sibérie*	crab apple
pruché, e	*rabougri*	crooked, stunted (tree)
quatre-saisons (f)	*hortensia*	four-seasons, hortensia
quenouille (f)	*roseau des marais*	bulrush, cat-tail
queue de renard (f)	*prêle des champs*	horsetail
rapace (m)	*bardane*	burdock
retiger	*reprendre*	to take, to sprout
rouget, quatre-temps (m)	*cournouiller*	dogwood
saint-joseph (m)	*pétunia*	petunia
saint-michel (m)	*petit sapin*	spruceling
sang-de-dragon, sang-dragon (m)	*sanguinaire*	bloodroot
sévigné (m)	*genévrier horizontal*	horizontal juniper
surette (f)	*oseille*	sorrel
talle (f)	*touffe*	clump (of bushes)
tourbe (f)	*(plaques de) gazon*	grass, sod

L'Argent (Money)

Canada	France	
cenne (f), cent, sou (m)		cent
une cenne, un cent, un sou		penny
un cinq-cents, un cinq-sous une pièce de cinq cents		a nickel five-cent piece
un dix-cents, un dix-sous une pièce de dix cents		a dime ten-cent piece
un trente-sous, un vingt-cinq cents une pièce de vingt-cinq cents		a quarter twenty-five cent piece
un cinquante-cents, un cinquante-sous, une pièce de cinquante cents		a fifty-cent piece
dollar (m), piasse, piastre (f) une piasse, une piastre, un billet d'un dollar		dollar, buck a one-dollar bill
un deux, un deux-piasses		a two
un billet de deux dollars		a two-dollar bill
argents (m,pl) (j'ai des argents)	argent	money
faire de la grosse argent	gagner beaucoup d'argent	to make a lot of money
argent de papier	papier-monnaie	paper money
être argenté	avoir de l'argent	to have money
baise-la-piastre (m)	avare	penny-pincher, miser
banque (f)	tirelire	piggy bank
banque à charte	banque privilégiée	chartered bank
en bas de	à moins de	(to buy sth.) for under
avoir des bidous (m)	être riche	to be rich
billion (m)	milliard	billion
blanc de chèque (m)	chèque en blanc	blank cheque
être bossu	être habile en affaires	to be a good businessman

Canada	France	
budgétaire (plan, termes)	à crédit	budget (plan, terms)
Caisse Populaire (Caisse POP) (f)	banque populaire	Credit Union
caler de l'argent	perdre de l'argent	to lose money
cash (m)	argent comptant	cash
payer cash	payer comptant	to pay cash
cassé, e	fauché	broke
casser	changer	to break (a bill)
cennes blanches	pièces de plus d'un "cent"	silver
cennes noires	pièces d'un "cent"	pennies
pas une cenne noire	pas un sou vaillant	not a red cent
change (m)	monnaie	change
changer (une piasse)	faire la monnaie de	to change (a dollar)
changer, encaisser un chèque	toucher un chèque	to cash a cheque
petit change	menue monnaie	small change
charger	demander; porter à son compte	to charge
charge (f)	frais	charge
chargeant, e	qui fait payer trop cher	expensive (store)
cheap	bon marché; de mauvaise qualité	cheap, inexpensive; cheap, shoddy
être dans le chemin	être en faillite	to be bankrupt
perdre sa chemise, se faire déculotter	perdre beaucoup d'argent, se ruiner	to lose one's shirt
chèque accepté, visé (m)	chèque certifié	certified cheque
chèque de voyage, chèque de voyageur	travellers (chèque)	traveller's cheque
chèque pas de fonds	chèque sans provision	N.S.F. cheque, bounced cheque
être chérant	vendre cher	to be expensive (store)
clair	tout payé	clear
coffre de sûreté (m)	coffre-fort	safe
coffret (m)		safety deposit box

Canada	France	
comment ça coûte?	*combien . . .*	how much does it cost?
de court d'argent	*à court d'argent*	short of money
être au débit	*manquer de fonds*	to be overdrawn
de dépense	*dépensier; cher*	extravagant; expensive
déposer	*déposer de l'argent*	to deposit money; go to the bank
échange (m)	*change, encaissement*	exchange (on foreign money, on cheque)
épargner, sauver de l'argent	*économiser*	to save money
dispendieux, ieuse	*cher*	expensive
faire bien sa vie	*gagner bien sa vie*	to make a good living
foin (m)	*argent, fric*	money, dough, bread
avoir du foin	*être riche, avoir du blé*	to be rich, well heeled
gager	*parier*	to bet
gagner cher	*gagner beaucoup*	to make a lot of money, to be well paid
hausse (f)	*augmentation*	raise
je n'ai pas un liard, pas un sou qui m'adore . . .	*. . . pas un sou vaillant*	I haven't got a red cent
(raisons etc.) monétaires	*pécuniaires*	monetary (reasons, etc.)
montant d'argent (m)	*somme d'argent*	amount of money
faire le motton, faire un motton	*gagner, trouver beaucoup d'argent*	to make, to win a bundle
être en moyens	*avoir les moyens*	to be in the money, to be a man of means
obligation d'épargne (f)	*bon du Trésor*	savings bond
octroi (m)	*subvention*	grant
avoir la palette; faire la palette	*avoir de l'argent; gagner de l'argent*	to have money; to make money
part (f)	*action*	share

Canada	France	
je vais payer pour	*je vais payer ça*	I'll pay for it
pour aussi peu que	*pour seulement*	for as little as
quêteux, euse	*pauvre*	poor, poverty-stricken
ramasseux, euse	*économe*	thrifty
réquisition (f)	*commande*	requisition
être dans le rouge	*être endetté, ne pas faire de profits*	to be in the red
séraphin, e	*avare*	stingy, miserly
faire son séraphin	être avare	to be stingy, to act stingy
être à serre, être serré	*manquer d'argent, être à court*	to be short of money
serre-la-cenne, serre-la-piastre (m)	*avare, grippe-sou*	miser, penny-pincher
se serrer la poigne (m)	*se serrer la ceinture*	to tighten one's belt
tête ou biche (bitche)	*pile ou face*	heads or tails
tomate (f)	*balle*	buck

Poids, Mesures, Quantités (Weights, Measures, Quantities)

Longueur (Length)

Canada

pouce (m) (″) (un quart de pouce, etc.)	inch (″) (one quarter of an inch, etc.)
pied (m) (′)	foot (′)
verge (f)	yard
brasse (f)	fathom
perche (f)	rod
stade (m)	furlong
arpent (m)	"arpent" (191.8 ft.)
mille (m)	mile
mille nautique	nautical mile

Superficie (Area)

pouce carré	square inch
pied carré	square foot
verge carrée	square yard
perche carrée	square rod
toise (f)	100 sq. ft.
arpent (m)	"arpent" (.85 acres)
arpentage (m)	number of arpents
acre (m,f)	acre
acrage (m)	acreage

Capacité (Capacity)

roquille (f)	quarter pint
demiard (m)	half pint

Poids et Mesures (Weights and Measures)

Canada	France
chopine (f)	pint
mouture (f)	1/10 peck
pinte (f)	quart
demi-gallon (m)	half gallon
gallon (m)	gallon
quart (m)	peck
boisseau, minot (m)	bushel
baril (m)	barrel

Mesures cubiques (Cubic Measures)

pouce cube	cubic inch
pied cube	cubic foot
verge cube	cubic yard
corde (f)	cord (of wood)

Poids (Weight)

gros (m)	dram
once (f)	ounce
once liquide	fluid ounce
livre (f)	pound
quintal (m)	hundredweight
tonne (f)	ton

Divers (Miscellaneous)

aux abords d'un pied	à peu près . . .	about a foot
assez (il est assez beau!)	très, tellement	very, so (Is he ever handsome!)
assez de (il a assez d'argent)	beaucoup de	a lot of
autant comme	autant que	as much as

Canada	France	
il a essayé autant comme autant ...	*il a eu beau essayé ...*	He tried ever so much, (but it didn't work)
il y en a un char et puis une barge	*... beaucoup*	There's quite a bunch, a whole lot.
batche de (f)	*paquet, fournée, cuvée*	batch (of people, bread, wine ...)
en bébite (Il fait chaud en bébite.)	*beaucoup, très*	very much, very (It's very hot.)
ben ben (C'est pas ben ben bon!)	*très*	very (It's not very good.)
botche (f) (d'oignons, de radis, de bananes)	*botte (oignons, radis), régime (bananes)*	bunch (of onions, radishes, bananas)
caisse de bière (f)	*boîte ...*	case of beer
(il travaille) en calice, en crisse, en grand, en gros, en maudit, en démon en tabarnacle ...	*beaucoup*	(he works) a hell of a lot
un calice, crisse, tabarnacle de bon film, un maudit bon film	*un très ...*	a damn good movie
canisse, canistre, canne (f)	*boîte*	can
rempli à capacité	*comble*	filled to capacity
carton (m), cartoune (f)	*cartouche*	carton (of cigarettes)
casseau, cassot (m)	*contenant pour les fruits, etc.*	basket for fruits, vegetables, carton for French fries, etc.
chaudiérée, seaudiérée (f)	*contenu d'un seau*	pailful
toute la chibagne (f)	*tout l'ensemble*	the whole shebang
en chien (ça fera drôle en chien)	*beaucoup, très*	extremely, very
cinquante (j'ai cinquante raisons pour ...)	*trente-six*	umpteen, a hundred (reasons)
comme tout (je t'aime comme tout)	*beaucoup*	a lot

Canada	France	
Comment loin que c'est?	*C'est à quelle distance?*	How far away is it?
une couple de	*quelques*	a few, a couple of
créte (f)	*caisse, panier*	crate
drum (m)	*baril, fût*	drum
égal (partager quelque chose égal)	*également*	equally
flasque (m)	*flacon; gourde*	bottle; flask
flesh, floche	*au même niveau; plein*	flush; full, crowded
fournée (f)	*gorgée*	mouthful
une gagne de	*une foule de*	a bunch of (people, things)
jarre (f)	*pot*	jar
en masse, en moses	*beaucoup*	a lot
à mort (je l'aime à mort)	*beaucoup, très*	a lot, very
paquet (de persil) (m)	*bouquet*	bunch (of parsley)
par (trois par huit)	*sur*	by (three by eight)
pesant, e	*lourd*	heavy
à plein, en plein (de l'argent en plein)	*beaucoup*	plenty of (money)
raide (cassé bien raide)	*tout à fait*	completely (flat broke)
sans bon sens (il boit sans bon sens)	*beaucoup; à l'excès*	a lot (he drinks a lot)
tapon (m)	*paquet*	bundle (of wood, paper, etc.)
ti (ti-Louis)	*petit*	little (for a person, kind of nickname)
en titi	*beaucoup*	a lot
toisage (m)	*mesurage*	measurement
trâlée (d'enfants) (f)	*bande ...*	bunch (of children)
tresse (f)	*régime (bananes), chapelet (oignons, maïs)*	bunch (of bananas, onions, corn)

La Date, l'Heure, le Temps (Date, Hour, Time)

Canada	France	
aux abords de cinq heures	*vers, près de*	around five o'clock, five hours
à chaque fois, à tous les jours, etc.	*chaque fois, tous les jours*	every time, day, etc.
a.m.; p.m.	*du matin; de l'après-midi, du soir*	a.m.; p.m.
8 heures p.m.	*20 heures*	8 p.m.
trois fois par année	*trois fois par an*	three times a year
asteur, asteure	*actuellement, maintenant*	now
les jeunes d'asteur	*la jeunesse actuelle*	the youth of today
aujourd'hui pour demain	*d'un moment à l'autre*	at any time
un autre dix minutes, deux heures	*encore dix minutes, deux heures*	another ten minutes, two hours ...
à l'avance	*d'avance*	in advance
d'avance	*vif, rapide*	fast (road or person)
avant-midi (m)	*matinée, matin*	morning, forenoon
dans l'avant-midi	*avant midi*	before noon
avoir, prendre de l'avant, être en avant	*avancer*	to be fast (watch)
mettre en avant	*avancer*	to put ahead
balance (f) (de la semaine)	*reste*	balance (of the week)
bretteux, euse	*musard*	dawdler
bretter	*musarder*	to dawdle
cadran (m)	*réveille-matin*	alarm clock
année (f), mois (m) de calendrier	*année civile, mois civil*	calendar year, month
cancellation (f)	*annulation*	cancellation

121

La Date, l'Heure, le Temps (Date, Hour, Time)

Canada	France	
canceller	*décommander, annuler*	to cancel
cédule (f)	*horaire, programme*	schedule
cédulé, e	*prévu, fixé*	scheduled
chaque trois jours	*tous les trois jours*	every three days
à coeur de jour	*toute la journée*	all day long
correct, e	*juste*	right (watch)
dans le cours de	*dans le courant de*	in the course of
à date	*à présent, à ce jour*	up to now, to date
mettre à date	*mettre à jour*	to bring up to date
en dedans de	*en moins de*	within, in less than
en dehors de (ses heures de travail)	*hors de*	outside of (his office hours)
le 8 de mars	*le 8 mars*	March 8
délai (m)	*retard*	delay
de suite	*tout de suite*	immediately, right away
le lundi d'ensuite	*le lundi suivant*	the next Monday
aux environs de cinq heures	*environ cinq heures*	about five hours
escousse (f)	*période*	period (of time)
une bonne escousse	*un certain temps*	quite a while
par escousses	*de temps en temps*	from time to time
éventuellement	*par la suite, plus tard*	eventually
fin de semaine (f)	*week-end*	weekend
en fin de semaine	*ce week-end*	last weekend; next weekend
en fin de février, etc.	*à la fin de, fin . . .*	at the end of February, etc.
focailler, foquailler	*perdre son temps*	to waste one's time
aller foulepine	*. . . le plus vite possible*	to go full out
être en frais de	*être en train de*	to be in the process of . . .
dans le futur	*à l'avenir*	in the future
Il est huit heures et cinq.	*Il est huit heures cinq.*	It's five past eight.
à bonne heure	*de bonne heure*	early

La Date, l'Heure, le Temps (Date, Hour, Time)

Canada	France	
As-tu la bonne heure?	*As-tu l'heure juste?*	Do you have the right time?
Il est huit heures dans 10 minutes.	*Il est huit heures moins dix.*	It is ten to eight.
Il est une heure moins quart.	*Il est une heure moins le quart.*	It is a quarter to one.
heure avancée		Daylight Saving Time
heure normale		Standard Time
plus de bonne heure	*plus tôt*	earlier
trop de bonne heure	*de trop bonne heure*	too early
aux petites heures	*très tôt le matin*	in the wee small hours of the morning
horloge grand-père (m)	*horloge de parquet, franc-comtoise*	grandfather clock
à l'année, à la journée longue	*à longueur d'année, de journée*	all year, all day long
à matin, à soir	*ce matin, ce soir*	this morning, tonight, this evening
hier au matin, hier au soir	*hier matin, hier soir*	yesterday morning, yesterday evening, last night
ce midi	*à midi*	at noon (today)
minute (je m'en viens! etc.)	*un moment . . .*	just a minute (I'm coming!)
mais que	*dès que; lorsque*	as soon as; when
par après	*après*	afterwards, later on
trois ans passés (je m'amusais)	*il y a trois ans*	three years ago (I was having a good time)
pendant une heure ᵣassée	*pendant plus d'une heure*	for over an hour
avoir une mauvaise passée	*passer par un mauvais moment*	to go through a rough period of time
patate, montre patate (f)	*montre qui ne fonctionne pas*	watch that doesn't work
il n'y a pas de presse	*il n'y a rien de pressant*	there's no hurry

La Date, l'Heure, le Temps (Date, Hour, Time)

Canada	France	
quand et (lui, etc.)	*en même temps que ...*	at the same time as (him, etc.)
quand que	*quand*	when
avoir, prendre du retard	*retarder*	to be slow (watch)
stage (m) (à ce stage-ci, je ne sais pas)	*stade*	stage
sur semaine	*en semaine*	during the week
au plus sacrant	*au plus vite*	as quickly as possible
sauver du temps	*gagner du temps*	to save time
une bonne secousse	*très longtemps*	quite a while
avant mon temps	*avant ma naissance*	before my time
depuis, pendant deux heures de temps	*depuis, pendant deux heures*	... two hours' time
en temps	*à l'heure, à temps*	on time, in time
en aucun temps	*en tout temps*	at anytime
dans les derniers temps	*dernièrement*	lately
de ce temps-ci	*en ce moment*	at the present time
il y a beau temps que	*il y a longtemps que*	it's been a long time since
jusqu'à temps que	*jusqu'à ce que*	until
être tout le temps ouvert	*être ouvert en permanence*	to be open all the time
par le temps que ...	*avant que ...*	by the time ...
Ça ne prendra pas goût de tinette.	*Ça ne prendra pas de temps.*	It won't take long. It'll happen before you know it.
tranquillement	*doucement*	slowly, easy
vite (adj.)	*rapide, vif*	fast, quick
vitement (viens vitement!)	*immédiatement*	quick, right away
zone horaire (f) (du Pacifique, des Montagnes, Centrale, de l'Est, de l'Atlantique, de Terre-Neuve)	*fuseaux horaires*	Time Zone (Pacific, Mountain, Central, Eastern, Atlantic, Newfoundland)

Fêtes et Congés (Celebrations and Holidays)

Canada	France	
(jour de) l'Action de Grâces (f)		Thanksgiving (Day)
Boxing Day, Après-Noël (m)		Boxing Day
Congé civique (m), Fête civile (f)		Civic Holiday
fête (f)	*anniversaire de naissance*	birthday
les fêtes, le temps des fêtes	*vacances de Noël*	Christmas holidays
joyeuses fêtes!	*bonnes vacances!*	happy holidays!
fête à la tire	*soirée où on fait le sirop de sucre*	sugar party
fêtailler, fêter	*nocer, boire, s'amuser*	to live it up, to drink, to have a good time
Fête de la Confédération (f), jour du Canada (m)		Dominion Day, Canada Day
Fête de la Reine		Victoria Day
Fête du Travail		Labour Day
L'Hallowe'en (f)	*veille de la Toussaint*	Hallowe'en
Jour du Souvenir	*anniversaire de l'Armistice*	Remembrance Day
jubilaire (m)	*personne que l'on fête*	person in whose honour a party is held
longue fin de semaine (f)	*week-end de trois jours*	long weekend
Lundi de Pâques (m)		Easter Monday
les Rois (m)	*Epiphanie*	Twelfth-day, -night
Saint-Jean (-Baptiste) (f), Fête nationale des Canadiens français (f)		Saint-Jean-Baptiste Day, French-Canadian national holiday
temps de Noël (m)	*époque de Noël*	Christmastime
valentin (m)	*carte pour la Saint-Valentin*	valentine

Jeux et Divertissements (Games and Amusements)

Canada	France	
accord (m)	*mise*	bet, kitty, pot
balancine (f)	*balançoire, escarpolette*	swing
se balanciner	*se balancer*	to swing
balloune (f)	*ballon; bulle*	balloon; soap bubble
donner la bascule à qn	*façon de fêter l'anniversaire de qn*	to give s.o. the bumps
bingo (m)	*loto*	bingo
jeu de blocs (m)	*jeu de cubes*	blocks
brandy (m)	*sorte de danse*	the "brandy" (a dance)
brasser (les cartes)	*mêler*	to shuffle (cards)
cabane à sucre (f)	*sucrerie d'érable*	restaurant specializing in maple syrup dishes
jouer à la cachette	*jouer à cache-cache*	to play hide-and-seek
câler	*réciter les figures d'une danse*	to call off (a dance)
câleur	*celui qui "câle"*	caller
un set câlé	*une danse "câlée"*	a dance with calling off
casseux de veillée (m)	*trouble-fête, le premier à quitter une soirée*	party-pooper, wet blanket
catin (f)	*poupée*	doll
catiner	*jouer à la poupée*	to play dolls
cochon (m)	*sorte de jeu de cartes*	"pig" (a card game)
corbeau dans la cage (m)	*sorte de danse*	"bird in the cage" (a dance)
danse (f) (aller à une ...)	*bal*	dance
danse carrée	*quadrille*	square dance

126

Canada	France	
discarter	*écarter; faire son écart*	to discard
doubler	*contrer*	to double (bridge)
enregistreuse (f)	*magnétophone*	tape recorder
épluchette (de blé d'Inde) (f)	*réunion, soirée en vue de décortiquer du maïs*	corn-husking party, corn roast
euchre, youkeur (m)	*sorte de jeu de cartes*	euchre
express (f)	*wagonnette pour enfants*	(child's) wagon
fêter	*faire la noce, s'amuser*	to celebrate
gigueur, gigueux (m)	*celui qui danse la gigue*	stepdancer
tirer de la jambette	*lutter par terre en essayant de se culbuter*	to Indian wrestle
machine à boules (f)	*billard électrique, flippers*	pinball machine
maître de cérémonies (m)	*présentateur, animateur*	emcee
marbre (m)	*bille à jouer*	marble, alley
musique à bouche (f), ruine-babines (m)	*harmonica*	mouth organ
musique western	*musique des cow-boys*	country and western music
party (m)	*surprise-partie, soirée*	party
passer les cartes	*donner les cartes*	to deal the cards
plain, pléne, slow (m)	*danse lente*	slow dance
tirer du poignet	*lutter à table en essayant de baisser la main de l'adversaire*	to arm wrestle
record (m)	*disque*	record
reel (m)	*air de quadrille*	reel, hornpipe
chanson à répondre (f)	*chanson à refrain*	a song in which the chorus is repeated by a group
set (m)	*danse de quadrille*	set (square dance)

127

Jeux et Divertissements (Games and Amusements)

Canada	France	
saut morissette, somerset (m)	*culbute*	somersault
soirée canadienne (f)	*bal du bon vieux temps*	barn dance, hoedown
souque à la corde (f)	*lutte à la corde*	tug of war
souigner, swinger	*faire pirouetter*	to swing (partners)
stepette (f)	*gigue*	stepdance
aller aux sucres, faire une partie de sucre	*faire une fête dans une érablière*	to have a sugaring-off party
survenant (m)	*qn qui arrive à l'improviste*	chance comer, unexpected guest
tague, taille (f)	*chat*	tag
toune (f)	*air de musique*	tune
tourne-disque (m)	*électrophone*	record player
turlute (f)	*air fredonné*	humming
turluter	*fredonner*	to hum
veiller	*avoir une soirée*	to have a party, a get-together
veillée (f)	*soirée*	(evening) party
veilleux (m)	*invité*	(party) guest
vite (m)	*danse rapide*	fast dance
violoneux (m)	*violoniste pour les quadrilles*	(old time) fiddler

Sports

General

Canada	France	
aréna (m,f)	centre sportif, palais des sports, stade	arena, rink
balle molle (f)	softball	softball
ballon-balai (m)	jeu qui ressemble au hockey sur glace	broomball
ballon-panier	basket-ball, basket	basketball
ballon-volant	volley-ball	volleyball
baseball (m)	base-ball	baseball
bâton (m)	batte	(baseball) bat
bâton, hockey (m)	crosse	(hockey) stick
billet de saison (m)	abonnement	season ticket
briser un record	battre un record	to break a record
camp d'entraînement (m)	lieu ou s'entraînent les joueurs avant la saison sportive	training camp
chambre des joueurs (f)	vestiaire	dressing room
club (m)	équipe	club, team
club-ferme (m), filiale (f)	équipe qui dépend d'une autre	farm club
coach, instructeur, pilote (m)	entraîneur	coach
colisée (m)	stade	coliseum
compte, pointage (m)	marque, score	score, scoring
compter	marquer, scorer	to score
compteur (m)	marqueur, buteur	scorer
conditions du ski (f)	bulletin d'enneigement	ski report
course sous harnais (f)	course attelée	harness racing
dépisteur, éclaireur (m)	prospecteur	scout
directeur gérant (m)	directeur	general manager

Canada	France	
disque (m), rondelle (f)	*palet*	puck
fiche (f)	*record*	record (of player)
football (m)	*football américain*	football
game, joute (f)	*match, partie*	game
gérant (m)	*directeur, manager*	manager
glissoire à tobagane (f)	*glissade*	toboggan slide
hockey (m)	*hockey sur glace*	hockey
hockey sur gazon (m)	*hockey*	field hockey
jeu de la crosse (m)	*jeu d'origine indienne*	lacrosse
faire du jogging, jogger, faire de la course à pied	*faire du footing*	to jog
joueur de baseball (m)	*baseballeur*	baseball player
joueur de football	*footballeur*	football player
joueur de hockey	*hockeyeur*	hockey player
le Toronto, le Canadien	*les Torontois . . .*	Toronto, Canadiens
ligue (f)	*championnat, division*	league
lutte (f)	*catch*	wrestling
nage (f)	*natation*	swimming
officiels (m)	*arbitres, juges*	officials
olympiade (f)	*jeux olympiques; compétition*	Olympiad
piste et pelouse (f)	*athlétisme*	track and field
pratique (f)	*entraînement*	practice
pro (m,f)	*professionnel*	pro
punir	*pénaliser*	to penalize
punition (f)	*penalty, pénalité, sanction*	penalty
quilles (f,pl)	*bowling*	bowling
repêcher	*prendre un joueur dans une ligue mineure*	to draft
repêchage (m)		draft
mettre au repêchage, offrir au repêchage		to put on waivers, to release
raquetteur (m)	*personne qui fait de la raquette*	snowshoer

Canada	**France**	
série mondiale (f)	*championnat professionnel de base-ball*	World Series
ski aquatique (m)	*ski nautique*	water-skiing
soccer (m)	*football*	soccer
squash (m)	*jeu de balle au mur*	squash
tenter	*dresser la tente*	to put up a tent, pitch tent
tobagane, traîné sauvage (f)	*toboggan*	toboggan
traîneau (m)	*luge*	sleigh, sled

Baseball

les positions   *positions*

(joueur d') arrêt-court (m)	shortstop
joueur de deuxième but	second baseman
joueur de premier but	first baseman
joueur de troisième but	third baseman
lanceur (m)	pitcher
receveur (m)	catcher
voltigeur de centre, joueur de champ centre (m)	centre fielder
voltigeur de droite, joueur de champ droit	right fielder
voltigeur de gauche, joueur de champ gauche	left fielder

autres joueurs   *other players*

coureur (m)	runner
coureur auxiliaire	pinch runner
frappeur (m)	hitter
frappeur auxiliaire, frappeur suppléant	pinch hitter
frappeur d'occasion, frappeur d'urgence	clutch hitter
joueur d'utilité (m)	utility player
lanceur de relève (m)	relief pitcher
lanceur gagnant	winning pitcher
lanceur perdant	losing pitcher

Canada

les coups	*hits*
balle fausse (f)	foul (ball)
ballon (m), chandelle (f)	fly
(coup de) circuit (m)	home run
coup retenu	bunt
coup sûr	base hit
double (m)	double
flèche (f)	line drive
grand chelem (m)	grand slam
roulant (m), roulante (f)	grounder, ground ball
sacrifice (m) (ballon sacrifice, etc.)	sacrifice (sacrifice fly, etc.)
simple (m)	single
triple (m)	triple

les lancers	*pitches*
balle (f)	ball
(balle) courbe	curve (ball)
balle glissante	slider
balle mouillée	spitball
(balle) rapide	fast ball
balle tombante	sinker
à l'extérieur	on the outside
à l'intérieur	on the inside
prise (f)	strike
tire-bouchon (m)	screwball

le jeu	*play*
attrapé (m)	catch
attraper, saisir	to catch
balle échappée (f)	passed ball
but sur balles (m)	walk
but volé	stolen base
claquer, cogner, frapper	to hit
croiser le marbre	to cross home plate
double jeu (m)	double play
élan (m)	swing
s'élancer	to swing
erreur (f)	error
frappe-et-cours (m)	hit-and-run (play)

Canada

le jeu	*play*
lancer	to pitch, to throw
lancer (m)	pitch, throw
Ligue Américaine (f)	American League
Ligue Nationale (f)	National League
manche (f)	inning
passe intentionnelle (f)	intentional pass, walk
Petite Ligue	Little League
points produits (m)	runs batted in
présences au bâton (f)	at-bats
retirer	to put out
retiré, mort	out
retirer sur trois prises	to strike out, to put out on strikes
être retiré sur trois prises	to strike out, to be struck out
être retiré sur décision de l'arbitre	to be called out
retrait (m)	out
retrait au bâton (m)	strike-out
sauf	safe
être déclaré sauf	to be called safe
glisser sauf	to slide in safely
triple jeu (m)	triple play
voler un but	to steal a base

le champ	*the field*
abri des joueurs	dugout
but, coussin (m)	base
clos de pratique (m)	bull pen
coussins remplis	bases loaded
cercle d'attente (m)	on deck circle
champ extérieur (m)	outfield
champ intérieur	infield
losange (m)	diamond
marbre (m)	home plate
monticule (m)	(pitcher's) mound
sentiers (m)	base paths
sur les sentiers	on base

Quilles (Bowling)

Canada

abat (m)	strike
allée, piste (f)	alley, lane
approche (f)	approach
boule (f)	ball
bowling, jeu de quilles (m), quilles (f,pl)	bowling
bowling (m), salle de quilles (f), salon de quilles (m)	bowling alley, lanes
bris écarté (m)	split
carreau (m) (carreau ouvert)	frame (open frame)
dalot (m)	gutter
feuille de pointage (f)	scoresheet
quille (f)	pin
cinq-quilles	fivepins
grosses quilles	tenpins
petites quilles	duckpins
quille-maîtresse, quille-reine	head pin, king pin
quilleur (m)	bowler
lancer (m)	throw
réserve (f)	spare

Curling

les joueurs / players

balayeur (m)	sweeper
joueur de curling (m)	curler
lead, premier (m)	lead
deuxième (m)	second
sous-capitaine, troisième (m)	third
capitaine, skip (m)	skip

la patinoire / the rink

cercle (m), maison (f)	house
cercle de douze, huit, etc. pieds (m)	twelve-foot, eight-foot circle, etc.
ligne de départ (f)	hack
ligne arrière	back line
ligne de la mouche	T-line

Canada

le jeu	*play*
ligne de jeu	hog line
mouche (f)	button
balai (m)	broom
blanchir un bout	to blank an end
bonspiel (m)	bonspiel
bout (m), manche (f)	end
Le cercle est vide.	The house is clean.
chasser une pierre	to take out a rock
Une équipe a une pierre-cible, deux pierres-cible . . .	A team lies one, two . . .
fermer la porte	to guard
fouetter	to clean out the house
frotter, raser une pierre	to rub a rock
garde (f)	guard (rock)
glace lente, rapide (f)	slow, fast ice
lancer, tirer une pierre	to deliver a rock
lancer vers l'extérieur (m)	out-turn shot
lancer vers l'intérieur	in-turn shot
marquer, réussir un point, deux points . . .	to count one, two . . .
mordeuse (f)	biter (biting stone)
pierre, roche (f)	rock
pierre blanche, rouge, etc.	white, red rock, etc.
pierre brûlée (brûler une pierre)	burnt rock (to burn a rock)
pierre-cible	shot rock
pierres gelées	freeze
placement (m)	draw (shot)
placer une pierre	to draw
faire ricochet	to hit and roll

Football

Canada

les positions	*positions*
aile (f), ailier (m)	end
arrière (m)	fullback
centre (m)	centre
demi-arrière (m)	halfback
flanqueur (m)	flanker
garde (m)	guard
plaqueur (m)	tackle
quart-arrière, quart (m)	quarterback

autres joueurs	*other players*
bloqueur (m)	blocker
botteur (m)	kicker
(demi-arrière, etc.) défensif	defensive (halfback, etc.)
demi de sûreté (m)	safety back
gagneurs de terrain (m)	ground gainers
joueur de ligne (m)	lineman
joueur au sol	rusher
(demi-arrière, etc.) offensif	offensive (halfback, etc.)
receveur de passes (m)	pass receiver

le jeu	*play*
attraper	to catch
attrapé (m)	catch
bloquer	to block
botté (m)	kick
botté de dégagement	punt
botté d'envoi, de reprise	kick-off
botter	to kick
échappé (m)	fumble
échapper (le ballon)	to fumble (the ball)
essai, jeu (m)	down
premier essai	first down
gains de 20 verges ... (m,pl)	20 yards gained ...
au sol	rushing
dans les airs	passing
hors jeu (m)	offside
intercepter	to intercept

Canada

le jeu	*play*
interception (f)	interception
mêlée (f)	huddle
passe (f)	pass
passe avant	forward pass
passe latérale	lateral
passer	to pass
plaqué (m)	tackle
plaquer	to tackle
retour de botté (m)	punt return
retour du botté d'envoi	kick-off return

le pointage	*scoring*
botté de placement, placement (m)	place kick, field goal
série au total des points (f)	total point series
simple (m)	single
converti (m), transformation (f)	convert
convertir un touché	to convert a touchdown
touché (m)	touchdown
touché de sûreté (m)	safety touch

le terrain	*the field*
ligne des buts (f)	goal line
ligne de mêlée	scrimmage line
ligne de trente verges, etc.	thirty-yard line, etc.
poteaux des buts (m)	goal posts

ligues	*leagues*
Ligue Canadienne de Football (f)	Canadian Football League
Ligue Nationale de Football	National Football League

Golf

aiglon, eagle (m)	eagle
aligner	to line up
allée (f)	fairway
aller (m)	front nine
atelier du pro (m), boutique (f)	pro shop
backspin, effet de rétro (m)	backspin

Canada

ballant, élan, mouvement (m)	swing
bâton (m), canne (f)	club
birdie, oiseau (m)	birdie
blaster, éjecter	to blast, explode
bogué (m)	bogey
bois (m)	wood
cadet (m)	caddie
caler, empoigner	to sink
carrosse, chariot (m)	cart
chalet (m)	clubhouse
chiper, cocher	to chip
chipeur (m), coche (f)	chipper
circuit (m)	circuit
claque, décoche, drive (f)	drive
claqueur, décocheur, driveur (m), grande canne (f)	driver
claquer, décocher, driver	to drive
cocher	to wedge
cocheur, fer plat, wedge (m)	wedge
coudé, dog leg (m), patte de chien (f)	dog leg
coup roulé, putt, roulé (m)	putt
faire un coup roulé, putter	to putt
coupe (f)	cup
départ, tertre (m)	tee, tee area
dérouter, shanker	to shank
coup dérouté, shank (m)	shank
drapeau, fanion (m)	flag
éclisse, slice, vrille (f)	slice
éclisser, slicer, vriller	to slice
effet mordant (m)	bite
effet accéléré, topspin (m)	topspin
fer (m)	iron
fer droit, putteur (m)	putter
fosse, trappe de sable (f)	sand trap
frais de jeu (m)	green fees
frise (f)	apron
grippe, prise (f)	grip
handicap (m)	handicap

Canada

herbe haute (f), roffe (m)	rough
lire le vert	to read the green
lisière (f)	fringe
marquer, spotter	to mark, to spot
masser, puncher	to punch
motte (de gazon) (f)	divot
normale (f)	par
omnium (m)	open tournament
parcours (m)	links
partie par trous (f)	match play
partie par coups	stroke play, medal play
pièce d'eau (f)	water hazard
pose (f)	lie
position (des pieds), posture, stance (f)	stance
poteau (m)	pin, stick
pousser (sa balle à droite)	to push the ball
punch (m)	punch shot
ramasser, retirer	to pick up
retour (m)	back nine
ronde (f), tour (m)	round
tee (m)	tee
terrain de pratique (m)	driving range
tirer sa balle à gauche	to pull the ball
topper	to top
tournoi-invitation (m)	invitational tournament
trou d'un coup, en un coup (m)	hole-in-one
vert (m)	green
vert d'entraînement, vert de pratique	putting green
voiturette (f)	electric cart

Hockey

les positions   *positions*

aile droite (f), ailier droit (m)	right wing
aile gauche, ailier gauche	left wing
avant (m)	forward
centre, joueur de centre (m)	centre

139

Canada

cerbère, gardien de buts, gauleur (m)	goalie, goal tender
défenseur, joueur de défense (m)	defence player, defenceman

autres joueurs — *other players*

couvreur, surveillant (de qn) (m)	(someone's) check
étoile (f)	star
gros canon (m)	big gun, high scorer
pointeur (m)	point getter, scorer
recrue (f)	rookie
tueur de punitions (m)	penalty killer
vétéran (m)	veteran

le jeu — *play*

attaque à cinq (f), jeu de puissance (m)	power play
dégagement illégal, dégagement refusé (m)	icing
dégager	to ice the puck; to clear the puck
donner de la bande, mettre en échec	to check
échappée (f)	breakaway
échec (m)	check, checking
échec arrière, échec avant	back-checking, forechecking
gauler	to play goal
hors jeu (m)	offside
immobiliser la rondelle	to freeze the puck
lancer	to shoot
lancer (m)	shot
lancer de revers	back-hand shot
lancer du poignet	wrist shot
lancer frappé	slapshot
mise au jeu (f)	face-off
passe (f)	pass
passer	to pass
pénaliser, punir	to penalize, to give (s.o.) a penalty
tricoter	to stickhandle

le pointage — *scoring*

aide, assistance (f)	assist
annuler, faire match nul	to tie

Canada

blanchir	to shut out
blanchissage (m)	shut-out
but (m)	goal
match nul (m)	tie
tour du chapeau (m)	hat trick

la patinoire — *the rink*

banc des joueurs (m)	players' bench
réchauffer le banc	to be benched
banc des punitions	penalty box
bande, clôture, rampe (f)	boards
cage (f), filet (m)	net
filet désert (m)	empty net
cercle de mise au jeu (m)	face-off circle
ligne bleue (f)	blue line
ligne du but	goal line
ligne rouge	red line
pointe (f)	point
rectangle du gardien (m)	goal crease
territoire (m), zone (f)	zone (defensive, offensive)

punitions — *penalties*

lancer de punition (m)	penalty shot
pénalisation, pénalité, punition (f)	penalty
punition de banc, d'équipe	bench penalty
punition d'inconduite, punition de mauvaise conduite	misconduct penalty
punition de match	match penalty
punition majeure	major penalty
punition mineure	minor penalty
pour assaut	for charging
pour avoir cinglé	for slashing
pour avoir dardé	for spearing
pour avoir donné un coup de coude	for elbowing
pour avoir fait trébucher	for tripping
pour avoir porté son bâton trop élevé	for highsticking
pour avoir retenu	for holding
pour échec au bâton	for cross-checking
pour obstruction	for interference

Canada

pour plaquage illégal	for boarding
pour rudesse	for roughing
pour s'être battu	for fighting

divers · *miscellaneous*

arbitre (m)	referee
Association Mondiale de Hockey (f)	World Hockey Association
bantam (m)	bantam
calendrier régulier (m)	regular schedule
clause de réserve (f)	reserve clause
coupe Stanley (f)	Stanley Cup
engagement (m), période (f), vingt (m)	period
juges de ligne (m)	linesmen
junior A, B ... (senior A ...)	junior A, B ... (senior A ...)
juvéniles (m)	juveniles
ligue mineure, majeure (f)	minor, major league
Ligue Nationale de Hockey	National Hockey League
match des étoiles (m)	All Star Game
match hors concours	exhibition game
match-suicide	sudden death game
midget (m)	midget
moustiques (f)	mosquitoes
officiel (m)	official
pee wee (m)	pee wee
période supplémentaire, prolongation (f), surtemps (m)	overtime
séries éliminatoires (f)	play-offs
temple de la renommée (m)	Hall of Fame

Les Sacres (Swear Words)

No exact English translations exist. The words given below vary in force. The indented entries are euphemisms corresponding to the original oath (e.g., *darn* instead of *damn*).

Baptême!
    Baptiste!
    Batêche!
    Bonguienne!
    Bonyeu!
Calice!
    Câline!
    Câline de binne!
    Câlique!
Calvaire!
    Calvasse!
Ciboire!
    Cibole!
    Ciboule!
Crisse!
    Crime!
Enfant de chienne!
Hostie!
Marde!
Mange de la marde!
Maudit!
    Maudine!
    Mautadit!
Moses!
Sacrement!
Sacrifice!
Sainte Vierge!
Tabernacle!
Tabarnac!
    Tabarouète!
    Tabernouche!
Taboire!
Torrieu!
Verrat!
Viande à chien!

Divers (Miscellaneous)

A

Canada	France	
O.K. d'abord	*Ça va comme ça.*	That's fine; O.K. then.
J'y vais d'abord.	*J'y vais alors.*	I'll go then. All right, I'm going.
d'abord que	*pourvu que; puisque*	as long as ; as, seeing that, since
Il faut aboutir.	*Il faut en finir.*	I have to get it over with.
abreuvoir (m)	*fontaine à boire*	drinking-fountain
s'accanter, se canter	*s'appuyer*	to lean against sth.
accaparant, e	*collant*	possessive (person)
achaler	*agacer, énerver, ennuyer*	to bother, to bug
achalage (m), achalanterie (f)	*agacement, énervement, ennui*	bother, nuisance
achalant, e	*agaçant, énervant, ennuyant*	annoying
adon (m)	*heureux hasard*	lucky break
Si ça s'adonne . . .	*Si cela se passe bien . . .*	If it works out . . .
Ça s'est adonné que . . .	*Il est arrivé que . . .*	It turned out that . . .
Je m'adonne bien avec elle.	*Je m'entends bien avec elle.*	I get along well with her.
Si ça vous adonne . . .	*Si ça vous convient . . .*	If it suits you . . .
être en âge	*être majeur*	to be of age
aider à qn	*aider qn*	to help s.o.
une fille trop en l'air	*une fille volage*	a flighty girl
avoir de l'air fatigué	*avoir l'air fatigué*	to look tired

144

Canada	France	
Fais de l'air!	*Va-t'en!*	Beat it! Scram!
prendre ça aisé	*en prendre à son aise*	to take it easy
Il se fait aller.	*Il se montre.*	He's showing off.
allô	*bonjour*	Hello, Hi
allumeur, lighteur (m)	*briquet*	lighter
Ça n'a pas d'allure.	*Ça n'a pas de sens.*	That doesn't make sense.
C'est plein d'allure.	*Ça a beaucoup de sens.*	That makes a lot of sense.
amancher, ramancher	*arranger, réparer*	to fix, repair
amancher une claque	*donner une claque*	to let go with a slap
être bien amanché	*être dans de beaux draps*	to be well off, to have a good set-up
être mal amanché	*être dans de mauvais draps*	to be hard up, in a bad way
amarrer	*attacher*	to tie together, tie up
ancien, ienne	*vieux jeu*	old-fashioned
à part de ça	*à part ça, d'ailleurs*	besides (that)
appointement (m)	*rendez-vous*	appointment
pas apprenable	*pas facile à apprendre*	hard to learn
attacher après qch	*attacher à qch*	to attach to sth.
Je suis après travailler, manger	*en train de*	I'm (in the act of) working, eating . . .
argument (m)	*querelle*	argument
J'en arrache asteur.	*J'ai des difficultés en ce moment.*	I'm having a hard time right now.
en arrière de	*derrière*	behind
en arrière	*à l'arrière*	to the back, rear
asseoir qn	*remettre qn à sa place*	to put s.o. in his place
s'assir (je m'assis, assis-toi, assisez-vous, je m'assisais)	*s'asseoir*	to sit down
s'assoupir	*prendre un somme*	to take a nap

Canada	France	
attendre après qn	*attendre qn*	to wait for s.o.
en autant que je sache	*que je sache*	as far as I know
en autant que tu diras . . .	*pourvu que tu dises . . .*	as long as you say . . .
nous autres, vous autres, eux autres	*nous, vous (pl), eux, elles*	we, us, you, they, them
nous autres mêmes, vous autres mêmes, eux autres mêmes	*nous-mêmes, vous-mêmes, eux-mêmes, elles-mêmes*	ourselves, yourselves, themselves
avoir su, . . .	*Si j'avais su, . . .*	If I'd known, . . .

B

avoir, faire la baboune	*bouder*	to sulk, pout
badloqué, e	*malchanceux*	unlucky
bâdrer	*ennuyer*	to bother
bâdrage (m)	*ennui*	bother
bâdreux, euse	*importun*	bothersome
C'est mon bag.	*C'est mon affaire.*	That's my bag.
barauder, barlander, berlander	*osciller; flâner*	to sway; to loiter
baraudage (m)	*allées et venues; flânerie*	comings and goings; loitering
faire du barda	*faire du tapage*	to make a racket
bardasser	*bousculer; faire du tapage*	to kick, push around; to make a racket
bardassage, bardassement (m)	*tapage*	racket
bardasseux (m)	*tapageur*	noisy person
Il lui manque un bardeau.	*Il est timbré.*	He's got a screw loose.
se faire barouetter	*être référé inutilement d'un bureau à un autre, etc.*	to get the runaround
barré, e	*étroit d'esprit; timide*	narrow-minded; shy
descendre en bas	*descendre*	to go downstairs
bastringue (f)	*bibelots*	knick-knacks
se faire passer au bat (batte)	*recevoir une râclée*	to get a spanking, licking

Canada	France	
être dans le même bateau	*être dans le même sac*	to be in the same boat
manquer le bateau	*manquer une occasion*	to miss the boat
bavasser	*bavarder, cancaner*	to gossip, to tattle
bavassage, bavassement (m)	*bavardage*	gossip
bavasseux, euse	*bavard*	gossipy; gossiper
baveux, euse	*insupportable, prétentieux; lâche; rapporteur*	snob, snot; chicken, coward; sneak
bébail, bye-bye	*au revoir*	good-bye
bébelle (f)	*chose; jouet; babiole*	thing; toy; knick-knack
être en bébite	*être mécontent*	to be in a stew
bec-fin (m)	*fignoleur*	fussy person, fusspot
bec-pincé	*prétentieux*	show-off
faire le gros bec	*faire la moue*	to pout
beignet (m)	*niais*	nincompoop
avoir en belle de	*être à même de*	to be able to
faire une belle	*se tenir debout*	to stand up (animal, baby)
rester bête	*. . . interloqué*	to be taken aback
dire des bêtises à qn	*. . . injures*	to insult s.o.
beurrer qn	*soudoyer*	to bribe
beurrage (m)	*pot-de-vin*	bribe
se beurrer	*se salir*	to get dirty
Bienvenue!	*De rien!*	You're welcome! Don't mention it!
avoir un blanc de mémoire	*avoir un trou de mémoire*	to have a memory blank
se mettre au blanc	*se mettre à découvert*	to stick one's neck out
avoir les bleus	*avoir le cafard*	to have the blues
blod, blood	*généreux*	kind, generous
se boquer	*s'obstiner*	to be stubborn
n'être pas sorti du bois	*. . . tiré d'embarras*	not to be out of the woods

Canada	**France**	
bomme (m)	*vaurien, voyou*	bum
bommer	*flâner, vadrouiller*	to walk around, bum around
être bon pour faire qch	*pouvoir*	to be able to do sth.
Ça n'a pas de bon sens.	*Ce n'est pas possible.*	That's crazy.
bonjour	*au revoir*	good day, good-bye
Il va du bord de Toronto.	*Il va du côté de Toronto.*	He's going towards Toronto.
Il est de mon bord.	*Il est de mon côté.*	He's on my side.
de bord en bord	*de part en part*	right through (clothing)
Il est fou sur les bords	*Il est fou par-dessus le marché; Il est un peu fou*	He is crazy to boot; He is a little crazy; He has a crazy streak
faire son boss	*se montrer*	to show off
bosser	*régenter*	to be bossy
botche (f)	*mégot*	butt (of cigarette)
tomber en botte	*tomber en ruine*	to fall to pieces
boucaner	*fumer*	to smoke
boucane (f)	*fumée*	smoke
faire du boudin	*bouder*	to sulk
bougrer le camp	*foutre le camp*	to take off, to leave
être dans l'eau bouillante, dans l'eau chaude	*être dans de mauvais draps*	to be in hot water
boulé (m)	*gaillard*	bully
bourasser	*rudoyer; être rude*	to push around; to be pushy
bourasseux, euse	*rude; maussade*	rough; bad-tempered
bourrer qn	*duper*	to fool s.o.
bozo (m)	*bouffon; niais*	fool; idiot
brailler	*se plaindre*	to complain, to bitch
braillage (m), braillements (m,pl)	*plaintes*	complaining, bitching
braillard, e	*qui se plaint*	complaining, bitching
brailleux, euse	*qui se plaint*	bitch, complainer
branleux, euse	*indécis; sur lequel on ne peut pas compter*	dawdling; unreliable

Canada	**France**	
braquer qn là	*planter qn là*	to leave s.o. standing there
brasser	*serrer dans ses bras; secouer*	to hug, squeeze; to shake up
bretter	*musarder*	to loaf
bretteux, euse	*musard*	loafer
amanchure de broche à foin, moyen de broche à foin	*moyen inefficace, primitif*	crazy, haywire way, stop-gap measure
faire, péter de la broue	*se vanter*	to show off, talk big

C

toute la cabane	*. . . maison, . . . camp*	the whole house (family)
cabochon (m)	*maladroit; étroit d'esprit, stupide; têtu*	clumsy; narrow-minded, stupid; stubborn (person)
cacasser	*bavarder*	to gabble
C'est pas un cadeau.	*C'est embêtant.*	That's some luck.
T'es pas un cadeau.	*T'es pas vivable.*	You're hard to get along with. You're no prize.
cailler	*être à moitié endormi*	to be half asleep
caler	*avaler; être pris; enfoncer*	to down (drink), to gulp down; to be stuck; to pull down (hat, etc.)
se caler	*s'enfoncer; se contredire*	to let oneself into (a chair), to settle into . . .; to contradict oneself
caméra (f)	*appareil-photo*	camera
canter	*incliner*	to tilt, slant
se canter	*se coucher, se reposer*	to go to bed, have a rest
On est capable.	*On peut le faire.*	Yes, we can.
Je suis pas capable de . . . , pas capable	*J'arrive pas à . . . , incapable*	I'm not able to, I can't . . . , unable
avoir le caquet bas	*avoir le cafard*	to feel low
casser	*cueillir*	to pick (fruit)

Divers (Miscellaneous)

Canada	France	
casser son français	*écorcher le français*	to murder French, speak broken French
casser sa pipe	*échouer*	to meet with failure, to blow it
catiche	*efféminé*	girlish, sissy
cauxer	*amadouer*	to coax
cave (m)	*dupe*	fool, stupid person
certain	*sûrement*	sure, of course
Il vient certain.		He's coming for sure.
chambranler	*chanceler*	to be shaky, stagger
chambranlant, e	*chancelant*	shaky, unsteady
prendre une chance	*courir un risque*	to take a chance
être chanceux, euse	*avoir de la chance*	to be lucky
Une chance que t'es venu.	*C'est bien que tu sois venu.*	It's a good thing you came.
parler à travers son chapeau	*parler pour rien dire*	to talk through one's hat
C'est pas les chars.	*Ça ne vaut pas grand-chose.*	That's not up to much.
charrier	*aller vite; chasser*	to go fast; to chase, throw out
chavirer	*déraisonner*	to go crazy, lose one's mind, talk nonsense
checker	*vérifier*	to check
chenu, e	*pauvre, vétuste*	poor, shabby
chiâler	*se plaindre*	to bitch, complain
chiâlage (m)	*plaintes*	bitching, complaining
chiâleux, euse	*qui se plaint*	bitch, complainer
(se) chicaner	*se disputer*	to argue, fight
chicane (f)	*dispute*	argument, fight
chicoter qn	*agacer qn; tracasser qn*	to irritate s.o.; to worry s.o.
avoir la chienne	*avoir peur; avoir le cafard*	to be afraid; to be down in the dumps
chieux, euse	*lâche*	cowardly, chicken
chiquer la guenille	*bouder; ronchonner*	to pout; to chew the rag

Canada	France	
se choquer	*se mettre en colère; se battre*	to get angry; to fight
chouenner	*blaguer; parler pour rien dire*	to joke; to talk nonsense
cliquer	*marcher, réussir*	to click, succeed, go off well
clou (m)	*sèche*	cigarette, smoke, weed
payer une coche	*payer cher*	to pay dearly
cochonnerie (f)	*saleté, désordre*	mess (dirty, untidy)
comme de fait	*de fait*	as a matter of fact
comme de raison	*naturellement*	of course
comprenable	*compréhensible*	understandable
comprenure (f)	*compréhension; intelligence*	understanding; intelligence
Ça nous connaît.	*On s'y connaît.*	We know all about that.
Il connaît pas mieux.	*Il n'est pas plus fin que ça.*	He doesn't know any better.
C'est pas contable.	*On ne peut pas le dire.*	You can't tell it (story). It's a secret.
connections (f)	*relations*	connections (in business)
se faire conter ça	*se faire réprimander*	to get told off
passer la nuit sur la corde à linge	*passer une nuit blanche*	to be up all night
être correct	*aller bien, marcher bien*	to be all right
C'est correct. Correct.	*Ça va. Entendu.*	It's all right. All right.
rendu au coton	*à bout de forces*	worn out, dead tired
Coudon! Coute donc!	*Dis donc! Mais enfin!*	Say! Look here! Come on now!
coulisse (f)	*trace*	streak (of paint, etc.)
C'est pas coupable.	*On ne peut pas le couper.*	You can't cut it.
courailler	*fainéanter*	to run around (in the streets, etc.)

Canada	France	
coureur de chemins (m)	*vagabond*	hobo, tramp
craquer	*lézarder*	to crack (wall, etc.)
craque (f)	*lézarde*	crack
Le lac est creux.	*Le lac est profond.*	The lake is deep.
dix pieds de creux	*dix pieds de profondeur*	ten feet deep
criages (m, pl), criaillage (m)	*cris, criaillerie*	shouting, whining, hollering
crinquer	*remonter*	to crank, wind up
être en crisse	*être fâché*	to be mad as hell
crisser	*lancer, foutre*	to chuck, toss
Je m'en crisse.	*Je m'en fous.*	I don't give a damn.
croche (m)	*malhonnête, voleur*	crook, thief
croche	*courbé, crochu, tordu; malhonnête*	crooked, bent; crooked, dishonest
tête croche	*qui a des idées fausses*	wrong-headed, mixed-up person
crochir	*devenir tordu; tordre*	to become crooked; to make sth. crooked
crochi, e	*tordu*	crooked

D

débarquer de qch	*se tirer de qch; se retirer de qch*	to get out of sth. (difficulty); to drop out of sth.
être débobiné	*être déçu*	to be disappointed, let down
débouler	*dégringoler*	to tumble down
se déchoquer	*s'apaiser*	to calm down
décoller	*filer, partir*	to take off, leave, scram
décrochir	*redresser*	to straighten out (sth. crooked)
définitivement	*sûrement*	definitely
se dégêner	*se mettre à l'aise*	to relax
démancher	*démonter; déplacer; démolir; aider qn*	to take apart; to move sth.; to destroy; to help s.o. out

Canada	France	
demander une question	*poser une question*	to ask a question
être en démon	*être fâché*	to be angry
dénomination (f)	*secte*	(religious) denomination
dépareillé, e	*sans pareil*	without equal, matchless
déparler	*divaguer*	to rave, ramble
ne pas dérougir	*ne pas s'arrêter*	to go on, continue, keep on going
se désâmer	*se fatiguer*	to wear oneself out
désappointer	*décevoir*	to disappoint
désappointement (m)	*déception*	disappointment
sans desseins (m)	*maladroit, sans initiative*	clumsy, dull-witted person
détoureux, euse	*rusé*	sly, tricky
détraquer	*perdre la raison*	to lose one's mind
D'où est-ce que tu deviens?	*D'où est-ce que tu viens?*	Where are you from?
dévoiler	*inaugurer*	to unveil
dévoilement (m)	*inauguration*	unveiling (of statue, etc.)
donner le diable à qn	*engueuler qn*	to give s.o. the devil
être en diable	*être fâché*	to be angry
n'être pas le diable	*n'être pas fameux*	to be no hell, not up to much
mener le diable	*faire du tapage*	to make a racket, raise hell
dis-moi pas que ...	*tu ne veux pas dire que ...*	don't tell me that ...
C'est pas disable.	*On ne peut pas le décrire. C'est extraordinaire.*	You just can't describe it! It's unbelievable!
domestique	*ménager; fait à la maison*	home (appliances); homemade
C'est pas donnable.	*On ne peut pas le donner.*	You can't give that.
passer tout droit	*ne pas se réveiller à l'heure prévue*	to sleep in, oversleep

E

Canada	France	
éberluant, e	*très surprenant*	amazing
s'écailler	*s'écaler*	to chip (paint, furniture)
écarter	*perdre*	to lose
s'écarter	*s'égarer*	to get lost, lose one's way
C'est écartant.	*On s'y égare.*	You can get lost there.
faire eau	*dégoutter*	to leak (bucket, etc.)
J'ai échappé mon crayon.	*. . . laissé tomber . . .*	I dropped my pencil.
C'est écho.	*Ça résonne.*	It echoes.
éclaireuse (f)	*guide*	Girl Guide
C'est écoeurant!	*C'est terrible!*	It's amazing! It's terrific!
écoeuranterie (f)	*saleté*	disgusting thing
écornifler	*fourrer le nez partout*	to nose around
écornifleux, euse	*fureteur*	nosy person, sneak
écrapoutir	*écraser*	to crush, squash
s'écrapoutir	*s'écraser*	to crash, fall down
écriveux, euse	*qui aime écrire des lettres*	a great letter writer
s'effoirer	*s'affaisser; s'écraser*	to collapse; to crash down
C'est beau, c'est effrayant!	*C'est terriblement beau!*	It's really nice! Is it ever nice!
Tu t'éjarres!	*Tu exagères!*	You're stretching it! You're going too far!
se faire embarquer	*se faire rouler*	to get taken in
embarrer	*enfermer*	to lock up
C'est embêtant.	*C'est embarrassant.*	It's puzzling.
Tu m'embêtes.	*Ça m'échappe.*	You've stumped me.
empigeonner	*jeter un sort*	to put a hex on
s'endormir	*avoir sommeil*	to be sleepy
s'enfarger	*trébucher; s'empêtrer*	to trip; to get jumbled up, confused

Canada	France	
se faire enfirouâper	*se faire maltraiter*	to get the short end of the stick
ennuyant, e	*ennuyeux*	boring
ennuyeux, euse	*qui a le mal du pays, nostalgique*	homesick
ensuite de ça	*après ça*	afterwards, later
entéka, en tout cas	*enfin*	anyway, . . . well, . . .
enterrer	*étouffer*	to drown out (sound)
envoie! envoueille!	*fais vite!*	come on! hurry up!
envoie fort!	*allez-y!*	go to it!
épeurant, e	*effrayant*	scary
à l'épouvante	*à la hâte*	quickly
n'être pas d'équerre	*être de mauvaise humeur; n'être pas d'accord*	to be in a bad mood; to disagree
à toute éreinte	*comme un forçat*	at a hard pace
prendre de l'erre	*prendre de l'élan*	to take off, get up speed
espérer qn	*attendre qn*	to wait for s.o.
à tout événement	*quoi qu'il en soit*	in any event
étrange (m)	*étranger*	foreigner, outsider
étranger (m)	*inconnu*	stranger
s'exciter	*s'énerver*	to get excited
excité, e	*énervé*	excitable, jumpy person
excuse, excusez	*pardon*	sorry, excuse me
Je m'excuse.	*Excusez-moi!*	I'm sorry.
C'est beau par exemple!	*Que c'est beau!*	Is it ever beautiful!
J'aime ça par exemple.	*J'aime bien ça.*	I really like that.

F

faire (bien)	*aller (bien)*	to agree with s.o. (food); to suit s.o.; to fit s.o.
faire fâcher	*fâcher*	to make angry
laisse faire!	*laisse tomber!*	forget it!

Canada	**France**	
Ça va faire!	*Ça va! Ça suffit!*	That'll do! That's enough!
ça fait que . . .	*alors . . . , c'est pour ça que*	so . . . , that's why . . .
fake, féke (m)	*chose truquée*	fake, sth. phoney
féker	*faire semblant*	to fake, pretend
fancy	*élégant, huppé, extravagant*	fancy, high-class
fantastique	*terrible, merveilleux*	fantastic, wonderful
farce (f)	*blague, plaisanterie*	joke
C'est une farce plate.	*C'est une mauvaise plaisanterie.*	It's a bad, stupid joke.
C'est pas des farces.	*C'est bien vrai.*	No fooling, **I**'m not kidding, **I** mean it.
Pas de farces!	*Sans blague!*	No kidding!
farouche	*craintif*	timid
fendant, e	*prétentieux*	conceited, smug, stuck up
feu (de forêt) (m)	*incendie*	(forest) fire
passer au feu	*être détruit par le feu*	to get burnt down
prendre en feu	*prendre feu*	to catch fire
fiable	*(qn) à qui on peut se fier*	trustworthy
donner son fiat à qn	*donner sa confiance à qn*	to trust s.o.
fier, ère	*orgueilleux*	proud, haughty
Je suis fier de te connaître.	*content de . . .*	I'm glad to know you.
film (m)	*pellicule*	film (for cameras)
fin, e	*gentil, intelligent*	kind, nice, intelligent
pousser des fions à qn	*insulter qn*	to dig, get at s.o.
flailler	*filer*	to fly, hurry away
flambe (f)	*flamme*	flame
flammèche (f)	*étincelle*	spark
flanc-mou (m)	*paresseux*	lazybones

Canada	**France**	
flâneux (m)	*flâneur*	loiterer
flauber qn	*rosser qn*	to beat s.o. up
flo (m)	*adolescent*	teenager
floche	*généreux*	generous, kind
focailler	*tâtonner*	to feel one's way around
focaillage (m)	*tâtonnement*	fumbling
fofolle	*folle; frivole*	crazy; frivolous
folleries (f)	*niaiseries*	foolishness, nonsense
avoir du fonne	*s'amuser*	to have fun
C'est le fonne.	*C'est amusant, drôle.*	It's fun. It's great.
pour le fonne	*pour rire*	just for fun
foqué, e	*foutu*	finished, done for
c'est forçant	*c'est dur, fatigant*	It's hard (work, etc.)
forum (m)	*colloque*	forum
faire un fou de qn	*duper qn, se moquer de qn*	to make a fool of s.o.
lâcher son fou	*se défouler*	to let oneself go, to let one's hair down
prendre une fouille, fouiller	*tomber*	to take a nose-dive
fourrer qn	*tromper qn*	to fool s.o., take s.o.
se fourrer	*se tromper*	to make a mistake
Je suis en frais de travailler.	*Je suis en train de travailler.*	I'm (in the act of) working.
faire son frais	*faire le prétentieux*	to act smart
prendre la fraîche	*prendre le frais*	to get some fresh air
franchement!	*vraiment!*	really!
frappé (m)	*snob*	snob
frapper un bon cours, etc.	*tomber sur . . .*	to find a good course, etc.
frapper une place	*arriver à un endroit*	to come to a place
fumage (m)	*action, habitude de fumer; tabac*	smoking; smokes, tobacco, makings
funérailles (f,pl)	*enterrement*	funeral

G

Canada	France	
Je gage que . . .	*Je parie que . . .*	I'll bet . . .
gagne (f)	*bande, clique*	crowd, gang
C'est une belle gamique.	*C'est une bonne combine.*	It's a good racket.
connaître la gamique	*connaître la musique*	to know the ropes
courir la galipote, galipoter	*nocer*	to run around, to gallivant
gaspil (m), gaspille (f)	*gaspillage*	waste
gaspiller qn	*gâter qn*	to spoil s.o.
garrocher	*lancer*	to throw, toss, pitch
se garrocher	*se dépêcher; se montrer; s'efforcer*	to fling oneself, rush; to show off; to try hard
un gars	*quelqu'un*	someone
gâté pourri	*très gâté*	spoiled rotten (person)
gelé, e	*drogué*	high, stoned
Il n'y a pas de gêne.	*Ne soyez pas gêné.*	Don't be shy.
gibelotte (f)	*affaire embrouillée, travail mal fait*	mess (situation, work)
gnochon (m)	*niais*	dumb-bell, idiot
gratter	*être mesquin*	to be stingy
gratteux, euse	*avare*	stingy person, tightwad
être gréyé	*être équipé*	to be set up, all set, well fixed
être mal gréyé	*être dans une mauvaise position*	to be in a bad way, badly off
grément (m)	*équipement, installation, nécessités*	equipment, get-up, set-up, stuff, rig
gribouiller	*se quereller*	to quarrel
être en gribouille	*être en chicane*	to be on bad terms
gricher	*crisser, grincer; pleurnicher*	to grind, to grate; to whimper
grichou (m)	*personne maussade*	sourpuss

Canada	France	
gringueux, euse	*avare; pauvre*	stingy, tight; poor
grippette (m,f)	*diable; enfant espiègle; personne sévère*	the devil; brat; strict person
faire la gueule de bois	*faire une gueule d'enterrement*	to sulk, have a low face
guidoune (f)	*femme de moeurs légères; femme de mauvais goût*	loose woman; a made-up, over-dressed woman, broad, floozey

H

J'haïs ça, etc.	*Je hais ça.*	I hate it.
haïssable	*espiègle*	mischievous
monter en haut	*monter*	to go upstairs
hein?	*pardon?*	eh? what?
hérisson, onne	*susceptible*	touchy
faire son homme	*faire comme un adulte*	to act grown-up

I

icitte	*ici*	here
faire son idée, se faire une idée	*se décider*	to make up one's mind
J'ai idée de faire ça.	*J'ai l'intention de . . .*	I intend to do that.
image (f)	*photo; statue*	picture; statue
importé, rapporté (m)	*étranger*	foreigner
insécure	*incertain, instable*	insecure
invitant, e	*hospitalier*	hospitable
itou	*aussi*	also, too

J

donner une jambette à qn	*donner un croc-en-jambe*	to trip s.o.
jarnigoine (f)	*intelligence, initiative; audace*	intelligence, initiative; nerve

Canada	France	
jaser	*bavarder*	to chat
jasant, e	*bavard*	chatterbox
jase, jasette (f)	*causette*	chat, talk
jeannette (f)	*jeune guide*	Brownie
joindre un club, l'armée	*s'inscrire à un club . . .*	to join a club, the army
jaune	*lâche*	yellow, cowardly
jomper	*sauter; s'enfuir*	to jump; skip work, run away
jongler	*réfléchir; rêvasser*	to think; to dream
jongleux, euse	*rêveur*	dreamer
(Ti-) Jos Connaissant (m)	*personne qui prétend tout savoir*	know-it-all
joual (m)	*français canadien populaire*	joual, very colloquial Canadian French
joualisant, e	*qui pratique le joual*	a joual speaker, writer, etc.
juste un café	*seulement un café*	just a coffee
C'est justement.	*Précisément.*	That's for sure. Precisely.

K

L'affaire est ketchoppe.	*C'est dans le sac.*	It's in the bag.
kodak (m)	*appareil-photo*	camera

L

lâcher	*abandonner*	to quit (sth.)
Lâchez pas!	*Courage!*	Hang in ! Don't give up!
Il lâche pas de travailler.	*Il ne cesse pas de . . .*	He doesn't stop working.
C'est un Anglais pure laine.	*C'est un vrai Anglais.*	He's a real Englishman, a dyed-in-the-wool Englishman.
Dites-lé! Faites-lé!	*Dites-le! Faites-le!*	Say it! Do it!

Canada	**France**	
lésiner	*hésiter; tergiverser*	to hesitate; to beat around the bush
lésinage (m)	*hésitation; tergiversation*	hesitation; beating around the bush
lever les pattes	*mourir*	to kick the bucket
licher	*lécher; flatter*	to lick; to flatter, to butter up
lichage (m)	*flatterie*	buttering up, soft soap
licheux, euse	*lèche-bottes*	soft-soaper, browner
limoner	*hésiter*	to hesitate
limonage (m)	*hésitation*	hesitation
limoneux, euse	*lambin*	s.o. who can't make up his mind
lisable	*lisible*	readable
liseux, euse	*liseur*	a great reader, book worm
littérature (f)	*dépliant*	literature (of a company, etc.)
lousse	*lâche; détendu; libre*	loose; relaxed; on the loose
lousse (m)	*jeu*	slack, play (in rope, etc.)

M

man (f)	*maman*	ma, mom
maganer	*abîmer, user; maltraiter; épuiser*	to bust, wreck, wear out; to treat badly; to tire out
mal-à-main	*incommode; désobligeant*	clumsy, hard to use, impractical; distant, unfriendly
à main	*commode; obligeant, accessible*	handy; helpful, right there when needed, etc.
mais que tu sois là	*dès que tu seras là, quand tu seras là*	as soon as you're there, when you come
Il est malade pour qch.	*Il a envie de qch.*	He wants sth. real bad.

Divers (Miscellaneous)

Canada	France	
malavenant, e	*hargneux*	cross, grouchy
malcommode	*pas vivable; indiscipliné*	hard to get along with; ill-behaved, bad
malendurant, e	*rude*	harsh, gruff
malin, e	*méchant*	bad, mean
mange-canayen, mange-chrétien (m)	*usurier, marchand qui demande des prix exorbitants; sans coeur*	shark, crooked merchant; slave driver
en manger toute une	*être réprimandé, rossé*	to get hell, beat up
d'une manière	*jusqu'à un certain point*	in a way
Je manque mes amis.	*Mes amis me manquent.*	I miss my friends.
marabout	*irritable, de mauvaise humeur*	grouchy
C'est pas marchable.	*C'est difficile de marcher par là.*	It's hard to walk through there.
prendre une marche	*faire une promenade*	to go for a walk
marlot (m)	*vaurien*	good-for-nothing
C'est marqué . . .	*C'est indiqué . . .*	It says (in the paper, etc.)
M'as te dire qch.	*Je vais te dire qch.*	I'm gonna tell you sth.
mature	*mûr*	mature
maudire	*jeter; abandonner*	to throw; to leave, drop
être en (beau) maudit	*être fâché, en pétard*	to be real mad
Ça parle au maudit	*Ça parle au diable*	It's out of this world. Fantastic.
pas pour un maudit	*pas pour un diable*	not for anything, the whole world
méchant, e	*mauvais*	wrong (number, address, etc.)
mélanger qn	*embrouiller qn*	to mix s.o. up, to confuse s.o.
mêler, mélâiller qn	*embrouiller qn*	to mix s.o. up
mêlant, e	*compliqué, embrouillant*	confusing

Canada	**France**	
mêlé, e	*embrouillé, perdu*	mixed-up, lost
mélâillage (m)	*confusion*	mix-up
Faut pas parler de même.	*Faut pas parler comme ça.*	You mustn't talk like that.
J'ai jamais vu une affaire de même.	*J'ai . . . pareille.*	I've never seen such a thing.
même à ça	*même dans ce cas-là*	even so
menterie (f)	*mensonge*	lie, lying
se mériter un prix	*gagner un prix*	to win a prize, etc.
Il prend du mieux.	*Il va mieux.*	He's getting better, recovering
minoucher	*flatter*	to butter up; to pet (animals)
avoir de la misère à faire qch	*avoir du mal à . . .*	to have a hard time doing sth.
manger de la misère	*passer par un mauvais moment*	to have a hard time
moé	*moi*	I, me
agir comme du monde	*agir comme il faut*	to act normal, behave properly
grand monde	*grandes personnes*	grown-ups
Dans le monde, qui t'a dit ça?	*Vraiment, . . .*	Who in the world, whoever told you that?
morviat (m)	*morvot; incapable*	gob (of spit); useless person, snot
être en moses	*être fâché*	to be mad, angry
C'est mourant.	*C'est marrant.*	It's hilarious.
mouver	*déménager, déplacer*	to move
se mouver	*se dépêcher*	to get a move on

N

être en nanane	*être fâché*	to be angry
prendre les nerfs	*s'emporter*	to lose one's temper
nerfé, e	*qui a du nerf*	nervy
habit neu	*habit neuf*	new suit
niaiser	*flâner, faire des choses insignifiantes*	to fool, kid, joke around

Divers (Miscellaneous)

Canada	France	
niaisages (m,pl)	*niaiseries*	horsing around, fooling around
niaiser qn	*se foutre de qn*	to make a fool of s.o.
nicagnac (m)	*bibelots*	knick-knacks
frapper un noeud	*rencontrer une difficulté*	to run into trouble, into an obstacle
Le nom est Jacques.	*Je m'appelle Jacques.*	The name is Jack.
Mon nom est Jacques.	*Je m'appelle Jacques.*	My name is Jack.
Quel est ton nom?	*Comment t'appelles-tu?*	What's your name?
crier des noms à qn	*injurier qn*	to call s.o. names
nono (m,f)	*imbécile*	nut, idiot
nounou, nounoune	*idiot*	nut
nounounerie (f)	*stupidités*	craziness
nuisance (f)	*incommodité*	nuisance

O

s'objecter à qch	*s'opposer à qch*	to object to sth.
C'est pas obtenable.	*Ça ne se procure pas.*	You can't get hold of it.
opportunité (f)	*occasion*	opportunity
C'est beau pas ordinaire.	*. . . extraordinairement . . .*	It's really, unusually . . .
originer	*prendre origine*	to originate
ostiner	*contredire*	to contradict
s'ostiner	*s'entêter; discuter*	to be stubborn; to argue
ostineux, euse	*entêté; raisonneur*	stubborn; argumentative

P

pamphlet (m)	*dépliant*	pamphlet, brochure
panel (m)	*groupe d'étude*	panel
paneliste (m)	*membre d'un groupe d'étude*	panelist

Canada	France	
panier percé (m)	*personne indiscrète*	gossip, s.o. who can't keep a secret
paniquer	*être pris de panique*	to panic
pantoute	*pas du tout*	not at all
paqueter	*empaqueter; faire (ses valises)*	to pack (package; suitcase)
être paqueté	*être comble*	to be packed, full
paqueton (m)	*havresac*	knapsack, pack
par ici	*ici, dans les parages*	around here
par exprès, par eksiprès	*exprès*	on purpose
par en haut	*là-haut*	up there somewhere
par rapport que	*parce que*	because
parade (f)	*défilé*	parade
paré, e	*prêt*	ready
pareil comme toi	*pareil à toi, comme toi*	just like you
Je t'aime pareil.	*Je t'aime quand même.*	I like you all the same.
Il n'est pas parlant.	*Il ne parle pas beaucoup.*	He's not very talkative.
parler comme du monde	*parler normalement*	to speak plain language, like everyone else.
parler en termes	*parler d'une manière affectée*	to use high-class, artificial language
parlure (f)	*parler*	speechways, ways of talking
prendre la part de qn	*prendre le parti de qn*	to stick up for s.o.
C'est pas partable.	*On ne peut pas partir.*	We can't leave.
être parti, e	*être ailleurs; être drogué*	to be out of it; to be high
Je n'ai pas vu personne.	*Je n'ai vu personne.*	I didn't see anyone.
passe (f)	*laissez-passer*	pass, free ticket
passer	*prêter*	to lend

Divers (Miscellaneous)

Canada	France	
être dans les patates	être dans l'erreur	to be on the wrong track
patente (f)	truc, machin	thing, whatchamacallit
toute la patente	tout le reste, toute la boutique	the whole shebang, all that jazz
patenter	arranger; inventer	to fix up; to invent
mettre la pédale douce	y aller doucement	to go easy, tread softy
pédaler	se dépêcher	to hurry, rush
peigne	pingre	stingy
C'est pas le pérou.	C'est pas le paradis.	It's no bed of roses.
peser sur un piton	presser un bouton	to press a button
piger	tirer au hasard	to draw (card, ticket, etc.)
pilasser qch	piétiner qch	to tramp sth. down
pilée (f)	pile	pile
piler	empiler	to pile up
piler sur les pieds de qn	marcher . . . ; déranger	to tramp on s.o.'s feet; to get in s.o.'s way
piloter qch	piétiner qch	to tramp sth. down
pas pire	pas mal	not bad
de pire en pire	de mal en pis	worse and worse
pis	puis; et	then; and
pissou (m)	lâche	coward
pitcher	jeter	to throw
piton (m)	bouton	button, knob
placoter	bavarder	to gab, gossip
placotage (m)	bavardage	gossiping
placoteux, euse	bavard	gossipy
plaisant, e	agréable	pleasant
se planter	s'appliquer	to apply oneself
plate	ennuyeux	dull, boring
C'est en plein ça.	C'est bien ça.	You're right on.
se faire pocher	se faire rouler	to get taken, tricked
être à la poche	mendier	to beg
pogner, poigner	attraper, pincer, prendre; émouvoir	to catch, grab, get; to get to s.o.

Canada	**France**	
On est pogné.	*On est complexé;* *On est pris.*	We are uptight, hung up; We're stuck.
se pogner après qch	*tenir à, se cramponner à qch*	to hang on to sth.
pousser des pointes à qn, pointer qn	*insulter, taquiner qn*	to make digs at s.o.
poisson (m)	*dupe, poire*	sucker, fool
C'est tout poqué.	*C'est tout abîmé.*	It's all wrecked.
se faire poquer	*recevoir des coups*	to get beaten up
portrait (m), pose (f)	*photographie*	picture
poser un portrait	*prendre une photo*	to take a picture
se faire poser	*se faire photographier*	to pose for a picture
possiblement	*peut-être*	possibly
poster	*afficher*	to post, put up (notice, etc.)
posteur (m)	*affiche*	poster
pratiquer son français	*s'exercer à parler français*	to practise one's French
pratique (f)	*exercice*	practice
Première classe.	*C'est parfait.*	That's fine. Swell. Terrific.
Ça me prendrait deux piasses.	*Il me faudrait ...*	I'll need two dollars.
Ça prend un professeur pour faire ça.	*Ça ne m'étonne pas d'un professeur.*	It takes a teacher to do that.
prendre par surprise	*surprendre*	to take by surprise
prendre pour, contre le Canadien	*être partisan ... , conspuer le "Canadien"*	to cheer for, against the Canadiens
mal pris	*dans de mauvais draps*	in bad shape, in a bad way, in trouble, up a tree

Q

quand que	*quand*	when
se faire passer un québec	*se faire monter un bateau*	to have one's leg pulled, to be sold a bum steer
faire ses quatre volontés	*faire à sa tête*	to do whatever one likes

Canada	**France**	
Il neigeait quelque chose de rare.	*. . . , c'était terrible.*	Was it ever snowing. It was snowing something awful.
à, en quelque part	*quelque part*	somewhere
Va queri (cri) le papier!	*Va chercher le journal!*	Go get the paper!
quétaine	*simpliste, vieille mode*	silly, backward, camp, corny
quétainerie (f)	*chose simpliste . . .*	camp, silliness, corn
C'est bien en quoi!	*C'est une raison de plus!*	All the more reason (to do sth.)

R

radouber, radouer	*réparer*	to repair
radoub, radouage (m)	*réparation*	repairing, major repairs
rapailler	*ramasser; rassembler*	to pick up; to gather, round up
à ras de	*près de*	near
raser de faire qch	*faillir faire qch*	to almost do sth.
ratatouille (f)	*fripouille*	rascal
faire le ravaud	*faire du bruit*	to make a racket
ravauder	*rôder, passer et repasser; faire du tapage*	to wander about, prowl; to make a racket
recevant, e	*hospitalier*	hospitable
rechigner	*pleurnicher*	to whine
rechigneux, euse	*pleurnichard*	whining
passer des remarques	*faire des remarques*	to make remarks
rembarrer	*enfermer*	to lock up
renforcir	*renforcer*	to strengthen, reinforce
ressoudre	*jaillir; arriver*	to squirt; to arrive
C'est le reste, le restant!	*C'est le comble!*	That's the last straw!
Il s'est fait retrousser.	*Il s'est fait remettre à sa place.*	He got put in his place.

Canada	France	
revirer	*détourner, tourner; faire changer d'opinion; retourner; retrousser*	to turn inside out, to turn; to change someone's mind, to convert, to brainwash; to return; to roll up (one's sleeves)
revoler	*gicler; être projeté*	to spurt up; to go head over heels, to be sent flying
entendre la risée	*avoir le sens de l'humour*	to have a good sense of humour
rôdeux (m)	*rôdeur*	prowler
roffe	*brutal, grossier*	rough
Roger-bontemps (m)	*sans souci*	good time Charley
rogne	*méprisable, avare*	despicable, greedy
se rouler	*se faire des cigarettes soi-même*	to make one's own cigarettes
rouleuse (f)	*cigarette qu'on roule soi-même*	hand-rolled cigarette, rollie

S

sa mère	*ma mère; ma femme*	my mother; the wife, the old lady
son père	*mon père; mon mari*	my father; the old man
mettre qn dans le sac	*rouler qn*	to cheat s.o., to put sth. over s.o.
sacre (m)	*juron*	swear word
être en sacre	*être en colère*	to be angry, mad
sacrer	*jurer*	to swear, curse
sacreur (m)	*blasphémateur*	foul-mouthed person
sacrant, e	*fâcheux*	annoying
sacrer son camp	*foutre le camp*	to take off
sacrer qn dehors	*foutre qn à la porte*	to kick s.o. out
sacrer un coup de poing	*foutre un coup de poing*	to give s.o. a punch
Je m'en sacre.	*Je m'en fous.*	I don't give a damn.
se faire passer un sapin	*se faire rouler*	to be had

Canada	**France**	
partir en sauvage	*filer à l'anglaise*	to go away without saying good-bye
scouincher	*éteindre*	to put out
scouinch (m)	*mégot*	butt (cigarette)
sentir chez le voisin	*espionner . . .*	to sneak, to spy on the neighbours
seulement que	*seulement*	only
shéker	*trembler*	to shake, tremble
siler	*pleurnicher; siffler, tinter*	to whine; to buzz, hum, whir
silage (m)	*bourdonnement*	buzzing
snoreau (m)	*enfant espiègle*	brat, smart aleck
souitcher switcher,	*transférer, changer de côté*	to transfer, switch
souitche, switche (f)	*transfert*	transfer, switch
steady	*permanent*	steady (job, etc.)
stime (f)	*vapeur*	steam
stone	*drogué*	stoned
straight	*pas dans le vent*	straight, square
suiveux, euse	*qui suit tout le monde*	sheep, follower
supposé (de)	*censé*	supposed to
aller su le père	*aller chez le père*	to go to dad's place
Il est sûr de venir.	*C'est sûr qu'il viendra.*	He's sure to come.

T

tanner	*fatiguer*	to tire
tannant, e	*fatigant*	tiring, tedious
un tannant de bel habit	*un très beau complet*	a hell of a nice suit
Je suis tanné.	*J'en ai marre.*	I'm fed up. I've had enough.
Je suis tanné de faire ça.	*Je suis fatigué de faire ça.*	I'm tired of doing that.
taper des mains	*applaudir*	to clap
se tasser	*se serrer, se rapprocher*	to move over, shift

Canada	France	
tata	*au revoir*	bye-bye (for children)
tatais (m)	*efféminé; niais*	sissy; idiot
tirer	*lancer*	to throw (stones, etc.)
tocson (m)	*homme têtu*	stubborn, bull-headed man
toé	*toi*	you
toffer qch	*endurer qch, tenir bon*	to put up with sth., to stick sth. out
toffe	*dur, difficile*	tough
toquer	*bousculer*	to bump against, push around
se toquer	*s'entêter*	to be stubborn
toutte	*tout*	everything
tout-suite, tusuite	*tout de suite*	right away
touche (f)	*bouffée*	drag, puff
traînerie (f)	*objet laissé à la traîne*	mess, thing left lying around
être traîneux, euse	*être négligeant*	to be sloppy, messy
trappe (f)	*piège*	trap
passer à travers qch	*tenir le coup*	to get through sth., make it through sth.
trempe	*mouillé*	wet, damp
tricoler	*tituber*	to stagger
trotteux, euse	*coureur*	gadabout
trouble (m)	*difficulté, ennui; dérangement*	trouble
avoir du trouble à finir	*avoir de la difficulté à . . .*	to have trouble finishing
être dans le trouble	*être en difficulté*	to be in trouble
truster qn	*avoir confiance en qn*	to trust s.o.
Il travaille-tu?	*Il travaille?*	Is he working?
L'eau est-tu chaude!	*Qu'est-ce que l'eau est chaude!*	Is the water ever hot!

V

Canada	France	
vacher	*paresser*	to be lazy, loaf around
C'est de valeur.	*C'est dommage.*	It's a shame, too bad.
varger	*frapper fort*	to hit hard, to wham
C'est pas vargeux.	*C'est pas fameux.*	It's not up to much. It's no great shakes.
versatile	*doué*	versatile
vider du coke dans un verre	*verser . . .*	to pour some coke into a glass
Viens-t'en!	*Viens ici!*	Come here! Come on!
Je m'en viens.	*J'arrive.*	I'm coming.
Il vient qu'il veut plus manger.	*Il lui arrive de ne plus vouloir manger.*	He gets so he doesn't want to eat any more.
avoir du visou	*avoir l'oeil juste*	to have a good eye, to be a dead-eye Dick.
J'ai mon voyage.	*Je n'en reviens pas. J'aurai tout vu. J'en ai assez.*	I can't get over it. Now I've seen everything. I've had it.

W

watcher	*surveiller, regarder*	to watch
Watche-toi!	*Attention!*	Watch out!
Wô!	*Arrêtez!*	Whoa!

Z

zarzais (m)	*nigaud*	imbecile
zigoune (f)	*sèche*	cigarette, fag